MODERN HEROINE
SOUL STORIES

24 REAL WOMEN
SOAR HIGHER
TO
GREATER HEALING
FORGIVENESS
TRUST
AND
STRENGTH

Contributing Authors Compiled By
Molly McCord

Spirituality University Press

Kindle ISBN 978-0-9965680-2-9
Smashwords eISBN 978-0-9965680-3-6
Paperback ISBN 978-0-9965680-4-3

Cover design and interior formatting by Lloyd Matthew Thompson
www.StarfieldPress.com

MODERN HEROINE
SOUL STORIES

FEATURING THE EXPERIENCES OF:

Isabella Aponte
Alison Baughman
Sharon Bright
Alice Brooking
Lady Beltane
Connie Cole
Erika Elmuts
Holly Faith
Lauren Goldstein
Hydee Hall
Diana "Dynasty" Hardy
Dominique Jaramillo
Sass Jordan
Debora Kiyono
Lili Krnic
Teresa Leming
Christine Lisio
Molly McCord
Lorraine Paul
Tamara Plant
Huntress Maxine Thompson
Brenda Quintero-Lombardi
Devon Telberg
Laren Rusch Watson

DEDICATION

We, the 24 authors of this book, share our personal stories with the intention of supporting other women improve their life story. 100% of the book royalties will be donated to Women for Women International (a U.S.-based non-profit organization) so more females around the world will be supported, educated, empowered, and trained to improve their daily lives in practical ways.

www.WomenforWomen.org

CONTENTS

SHE CONNECTS

.

INTRODUCTION

As she leaned over to inhale a blossoming young flower, Persephone felt a quiet inner joy as the expansive valley around her burst with colors. The morning air was young and clear as she selectively picked the white narcissus, a springtime bloom with tall, thin stems and skinny petals. She stuck one floret behind her right ear, a stark contrast of light against her long mane of dark, silky hair. Her navy blue dress bellowed in the gentle breeze; her mind was focused on the simple task at hand. The sun's marigold rays grew wider, yet she was in no rush as her wicker basket grew heavier in bounty. She was enjoying a time of tranquility and earthly fertility. Persephone was so consumed with her morning ritual and the peace of the land that she had no idea something darker was lurking right under her bare feet — literally.

Low and behold, our fair maiden was quickly surrounded by an unexpected darkness in the form of a grumpy, hard fellow named Hades, the Lord of the Underworld. He was enraptured with her beauty, softness, and charms; he wanted to possess her sweetness and light as his own. When Hades saw Persephone alone in the field on this springtime morn, he didn't exactly pause to thoughtfully consider whether his next actions were a good choice, or what the long-term consequences may be, or the moral implications of kidnapping someone against their will. Nah, Hades did not exactly operate with the highest level of awareness. As the Undertaker of the Dead and Darkness, Hades just took what he wanted, when he wanted it. And on that day, he wanted this young woman to be his new bride.

Before Persephone could fathom what was happening, the ground below her cracked open with Hades' Underworld powers and she was swiftly grabbed from her joy-filled task. Her basket full of innocent petals were tossed wildly into the wind, and were abruptly scattered across the field in a mess of chaos. Persephone was quickly dragged down into the depths of Hades' lair through the rocky opening in the earth. She tumbled blindly and helplessly into his realm of darkness and dread.

Then just as quickly, the fissure in the land melded back together seamlessly. Silence prevailed. The earth was then forever changed as the young Goddess of Agriculture went missing. Persephone had vanished from the light.

Well, dang it. Talk about a great morning that headed downhill fast. Poor Persephone had no idea her peaceful life would take such a drastic turn in an instant by an unknown jerk.

Safe to say, none of us live in a simple Greek myth these days. Our minds are scattered with any number of rotating daily needs and responsibilities. We wake up to guzzle coffee and get out the door, then race through the day's priorities with one hand tapping on our phones, and the other trying to compose emails or post on social media. By comparison, it would be amazing to enjoy even a few hours of peace wandering in a field of flowers.

So what is relevant to us today about this Greek myth? It is the deeper symbolism of Persephone's tale that is highly pertinent in our modern existence. Life can be humming along as we know it, as predictable as a spinning wheel, and then unexpectedly, something comes from out of the blue and shakes us at our core. We are yanked from our normal existence because of a life-changing email. A shocking phone call. A swift development. An unexpected diagnosis. A hard decision. A life-changing event. An unravelling of what you had kept inside; tight and secure in a safe place that was now suddenly exposed and raw. A loved one's death.

Or perhaps there is no immediate event that grabs you into its wrath. Instead, it is a slow, growing awareness that a part of you is suffocating, or struggling, or being challenged in increasingly uncomfortable ways. A small hurt has expanded into an unavoidable chronic ache. A deep knowingness can no longer be ignored. A small part of yourself has been screaming for your attention, and now you must truly listen to it as the yells escalate in volume. A truth you have suppressed must be released. *Something has to change for you.*

Whatever it may be, or however it shows up, one thing is inescapable: something bigger than "life as you know it" is calling for your soul's attention. You are being pushed from one experience of your life into another unknown territory that is challenging, hard, or deeply emotional. Whether that change happens quickly or slowly, a new journey begins down into the depths of your own energy and inner world.

In the following chapters, you are going to meet 24 women who did just that. Through four soul themes—Spiritual Awakenings and Growth; Owning Her Power; Health, Healing and Well-being; and Soul Mates and Relationships— each woman tells her story of being pulled into something greater and more powerful than she had ever known before. From divorce, professional setbacks, love connections, friendships ending, and questioning her life direction; to health challenges, losing her mom, becoming a mom, moving through inner pain, financial fears, and many more topics, all are shared as open, heart-based, and modern-day passages into greater soul growth. Each author shares her fears, emotional depths, doubts, pain, and struggles. She takes you into parts of her experiences that have been held private and sacred. She opens up to express her fears and vulnerabilities. She leaves behind an old definition of self that has expired; the innocent part of her life before she had to journey into more of herself than ever before.

Just as Persephone was dragged unexpectedly away from her bliss, you'll witness how each woman also had to move away from her "normal" life as something changed her at her core. She became her own Modern Heroine because she moved through a personal, spiritual journey that expanded her definition of self.

Is there one singular type of heroine journey? Of course not. The stories are as varied and diverse as each person on the planet. Yet in this collection, they have significant overlaps and intersections that intertwine into eight characteristics:

1. It is solo. She does it by herself, for herself.

2. It is unknown. She moves outside of a comfort zone to find herself.
3. It tests her limits. She is pushed by external circumstances.
4. It is emotional. She experiences the full spectrum of her inner world.
5. It is transformational. She experiences a death and rebirth of herself.
6. It is risky. She is required to leap somehow: emotionally, spiritually, financially, mentally, psychologically.
7. It is comprehensive. She moves through a full process of unconsciousness to greater consciousness.
8. It is a permanent and significant change in self-identity. She becomes more of her Soul self and cannot go back to who she was previously.

What makes a Modern Heroine different from a mythical one, besides those pesky Underworld villains? One answer is consciousness. She has the ability to see into herself on deeper levels; to understand her experience psychologically; to ask deeper, more probing questions about what she is learning as a soul in human form.

More than ever, we have the ability in our modern age to expand our consciousness around the struggles, pain, and challenges in our lives. We have access to more teachers, resources, videos, guides, books, and teachings than ever before that can help us see where we are being encouraged to grow, trust, heal, and forgive in deeper ways. We can see how our power is ours to claim and activate on deeper levels. We can allow ourselves the room to feel deeply and emote truthfully, and then pull it all together and put on her big girl pants and sassy heels to march back out into the world with greater confidence and strength. No one else can make her a heroine except herself. And she is never a victim.

The idea for this collection of stories came about through unexpected means, as many creative projects often do: *Modern Heroine Soul Stories* was birthed from the unexpected popularity of my second book, *The Modern Heroine's Journey of Consciousness*. Thousands upon thousands of women resonated with the journey of spiritual growth that I shared in that guidebook. As I listened to women on social media and email express how strongly they knew this path, too, it became abundantly clear that something bigger could be created to connect with even more people. All of these contributing authors share their personal journey with the intention of opening, inviting, and connecting you to a bigger understanding of strength, trust, healing, and forgiveness in your own life.

And heads up: we are real, everyday women who swear at times, get brutally honest, speak with ownership, and dance in the shadows of our own inner darkness. You are being invited into stories that are being fully expressed for the first time. We are going to be vulnerable and raw with you—and truthfully, we would have it no other way.

Then another idea came through about this project. When stirring messages hit a popular chord, not only can we bring *in* more people to contribute their experiences, but I believe we can also give more *out* into the world, as well. With that intention, all royalties from this book are being donated to a United States-based non-profit organization called Women for Women International. Since 1993, Women for Women

International has helped more than 462,000 marginalized women in eight countries affected by war and conflict by offering support, tools, and access to life-changing skills. These resources help them move from crisis and poverty, to stability and economic self-sufficiency. Women attend weekly or bi-weekly training classes in their communities to learn about business, finances, basic education, literacy, and understanding their civil rights as fundamental ways to improve herself, her family, and her community for long-term growth.

We are 24 women from all over the globe sharing our personal stories to help more women improve their life stories in practical ways with the royalties from this book.

Now, not to ruin the ending of Persephone's myth, but our girl did not stay with Hades in the Underworld for the rest of her life. Her unexpected voyage into the dark only made her more powerful, just as a Modern Heroine digs deeper into her own power, choices, and self to re-emerge as a more authentic and real version of her true self. More about how Persephone's adventure unfolded will be shared on the other side of our 24 soul stories.

We began with the mythical tale of Persephone to highlight how life can grab us and yank us deeper into our unconscious selves in order to return us back to the world as a more fully conscious person on the other side. When myth and modern are woven together, we find longstanding, universal messages that can unite us through shared themes and invite us to open up more to one another.

What if you weren't alone during one of your life's biggest turning points?

What if one of your most private vulnerabilities was

actually the best possible connection point with other women?

What if another woman—whom you have never met in person—could relate to your most private experiences like a true sister?

Perhaps you will meet her in one of these stories. We hope you find inspiration, strength, and perhaps even a little bit of yourself in this book.

We'll begin our journey together with the first theme of Spiritual Awakenings and Growth as seven women share how they started to see and feel more of their connection to the Universe/God/Source, and accessed their inner gifts, talents, and healing intentions.

Onwards we journey out, down, and back up to the light.

Molly McCord, M.A.
Author, Spiritual Teacher, Business Guide

"The Modern Heroine's Journey of Consciousness is unique to each woman based on what she is here to learn, master, complete, balance, and heal at a Soul level."

The Modern Heroine's Journey of Consciousness by Molly McCord
Book Two in The Awakening Consciousness Series

SHE AWAKENS

{ Spiritual Awakenings and Growth }

"She may not feel completely ready, or absolutely
certain, or totally convinced about what to do or how to
do it perfectly.
But she knows it is time.
She has to go for it.
She is ready to trust the feelings as messages of faith.
It is time to answer the Call of her Soul.
She jumps."

The Modern Heroine's Journey of Consciousness

SHE FINDS HER CONNECTION
TO THE UNIVERSE

By Tamara Plant

The first time I tapped into the Universe and planted the seeds of intention, I had no idea that I was tapping into the Universe and planting seeds of any kind. I was 20 years old and had just been politely asked to leave college in the third semester of a four-semester journalism program. It might have had something to do with skipping all the core classes that held absolutely no appeal to me because, in my opinion, they could not open any doors towards becoming the superstar sports reporter I knew I was going to be. At the time, my ego took a hit, but I knew I'd be fine, with or without that damn diploma.

"Confidence doesn't mean you're any good," my professor said.

I had survived worse than hearing that truth. Growing up in the inner city teaches you resilience and toughens you through lessons of violence, poverty, and fear. I left home when I was 16 years old, but I would have left sooner if I'd had the opportunity. I didn't want to end up like my mom, who was living on welfare and in an abusive relationship. I didn't want to wake up with drug dealers and prostitutes on my couch, and I sure as hell didn't want to be too scared to go to sleep anymore.

I didn't have much when I was growing up, but I had my dreams and, somehow, I knew they would all come true. Words would flow when I was writing, almost as if they were whispered to me and I was simply the conduit. I had to be practical, though, because I was certain there was no money in becoming an author. There was definitely a job with money in journalism, though, so I took that path. I focused my sights on becoming a sports writer and working for a daily paper. The only step I knew to take was to go to college, but even then I had no idea how to apply.

At 19 years old, I was living on my own just a few blocks from where I grew up, but far enough away from the inner city to feel like I'd moved to a different country. In my short life, I'd seen my mom beaten physically, emotionally, and mentally more times than I'd seen the sun rise. Almost every house we moved out of was condemned and torn down right after we left. When I was 11, my step dad decided he could touch me wherever and whenever he wanted. My favorite uncle overdosed when I was 12, and a handful of other relatives died tragic deaths. I was homeless when I was 17. My beautiful grandma passed away from cancer when I was 19; she was 57. I had no idea how to live without pain and loss; it had always been my normal. So I buried it and decided to be laser-focused on becoming a writer.

Getting into college was easier than I thought it

would be, but getting kicked out was harder than I had ever imagined. There was no way I'd ever let anyone know how devastated I was, not even my professor who thought that insulting me would break me.

I simply looked for another way to make my dreams come true.

I took a freelancing job writing for a local sports rag that was published once a month and distributed on "Take One" racks around the city. It didn't matter that I was making $50 for each column I wrote and could only submit two columns per month, or that I was making $5.25 an hour at a part-time retail job. I was on my own and doing something to make my dreams come true. Looking back, it was all a trail of breadcrumbs on this path to living the life I thought I wanted, but at the time I was depressed, broke, and wondering why the hell nothing was working out for me. I couldn't sever ties with my past. I kept returning to the inner city to reconcile some piece of my fractured relationship with my mom. Yet every time I left her, I felt worse than ever because she was making choices that kept her in a downward spiral.

As for romantic relationships, well forget about it. There was one guy I let my guard down with and was allowing him to get close to me. We had known each other for three months and spent as much time talking as we could, getting to know everything about one another. It was a long-distance relationship with a series of phone calls and long nights slowly sharing as much as humanly possible.

The night before my 22nd birthday, he called to ask if I'd received my present and I smiled.

"I did!"

It was a black and white striped stuffed tiger with a

card that read, "Happy Birthday, Tamara. Love, Keon."

A simple note, but it meant everything to me. I hadn't heard the word "love" in years and I wasn't sure of the context, so I asked.

"Why did you sign it that way?"

"Because I think I'm falling in love with you," he said.

I wasn't sure what to do with that even though I felt the same way. Love wasn't something I was comfortable with, yet all I could think of was, "Me too!"

Instead I barely whispered, "I feel the same way."

We hung up shortly after and I wish I had known that would be our last conversation. He died five days after my birthday from an epileptic seizure. I only found out because I kept calling but he never returned my calls. It wasn't until his mom answered the phone, and asked, "Are you the girl in the picture?"

My heart shattered into a million pieces and I was convinced there was some twisted Universal Law that said, "When one good thing happens to you, ten bad things happen to balance it all out." And because I believed it to be true, so it was.

That summer, I went to visit my grandma's grave and told her about my life. Three years had passed since her death, but I still felt her presence. The more I told her about how things were unfolding, the more I broke down, sobbing. I was sick of people dying or leaving me. I was tired of feeling like I'd never break the cycle my mom had created. Most of all I was alone in the world and it seemed like there was nothing I could do about it.

I collapsed in a heap beside her grave, shaking and letting it all pour out: the pain, the grief, and the soul-crushing weight I had been carrying. Without even knowing what I was doing, I released it all to the

Universe and my guardian angels.

My head hurt and my eyes were red, but I felt a cathartic light fill my entire being. I left the grave site knowing exactly what I had to do to change the direction of the path I was on. I had to leave this place. I couldn't keep repeating the same mistakes and making the same choices if I expected anything different to happen.

Without knowing I was about to co-create some magic with the Universe, I planted seeds of intention by envisioning the life I had always dreamed of. I saw myself in a newsroom chatting with other sports writers and laughing about how easy it was to make my dreams come true. I pictured myself having coffee and listening to music, grateful for the life I was living but that wasn't enough to make it a reality. Something inside me told me I needed to take action in order to really stir up the Universal magic and get shit going. So a few weeks later, I went to the library and scanned the newspapers that were on display. I asked myself where I would want to live, if I could live anywhere. My eyes immediately were drawn to a Canadian newspaper, *The Okanagan Sun*. I had no idea where that was but it sounded like heaven compared to the inner city I kept returning to. I wrote down the contact information from the newspaper and went home to figure out what to do with it.

There was no obvious sign from the Universe to apply for a job other than my intuition, and even then, I didn't know that I was using it. There wasn't a job posting or anything to indicate that they would be looking for someone to write for them, so I drafted an email introducing myself to the sports editor and told him why he needed me to be a part of his team. He replied letting me know they weren't hiring at that time but he would keep my information on file. It was disappointing, but I was used to it (see what I did there? I was so used to being disappointed that I kept attracting it without realizing it). I shrugged it off and resigned myself to living a life of struggle and disappointment. I gave up and again, without knowing it, surrendered to the Universe. I went on with my life, working to make ends meet and making bad choices at nightclubs to pass the time.

Every once in a while, a song lyric would catch my attention, and I'd think it was a message from my grandma or my boyfriend—but that was stupid, right? Yet I couldn't ignore the song messages when they would repeat at the strangest times in the weirdest places, so eventually I started paying attention to them. I didn't know why, but the lyrics were almost like secret whispers to keep going and know that I was never alone.

Two weeks later, I got a voicemail from the sports editor at *The Okanagan Sun*, who also edited a sister newspaper, *The Daily Courier*.

"Hey Tamara, a job just opened up. Do you have time to chat next week? Give me a call and we'll talk."

I couldn't believe my luck! Hell yeah, I had time to talk!

After the phone interview, he sent an email asking me to fly out for a second meeting. I had never been to Kelowna, British Columbia, but as the plane descended, it felt like home, like I was meant to be there. I also realized it was the magical place from my childhood that I'd dreamed of going to visit because it was the home of Flintstones Bedrock City, a theme park I'd only seen in commercials. It was another perfect example of the manifesting I had no idea I was doing.

Not gonna lie—I thought I totally bombed the interview. I had to write an article about the local football team and my lead was something stupid like, "Scratch and sniff, right here. Smell that? It smells like team spirit!"

Ugh, that still makes me cringe. I thought I was so clever with that dorky lead, playing on the "Smells Like Teen Spirit" song by Nirvana. I left wishing I had another chance to impress them, but I still felt confident about the rest of the interview. I knew I was a good writer, and I knew I was blazing some trails as one of a handful of female sports reporters in Canada. I just needed some time to prove it.

When I returned home, I decided that the only way to move forward with my life was to close the chapter on my past. It had been almost a year since Keon's death, so I flew out to meet his mom and say goodbye to him for good. It was like ripping my heart open again, but the love I felt from his mom made it worth it. When I got home, there was a message on my answering machine.

"Hey Tamara, it's Mark from *The Daily Courier*. We want you to start immediately if you can. Give me a call back and we'll discuss the details. Looking forward to it!"

The Universe had a plan and I was beginning to have some faith. I still didn't understand that I was the one who could change my life by trusting the Universe or manifesting dreams, but I didn't need Deepak Chopra or Louise Hay to tell me the secrets of the Universe. What I needed was to start trusting my instincts and realizing that I was trapped in my head, not in my circumstances.

Once I let go of everything I "knew" and tapped into everything I *knew*, the Universe took my hand and led the way.

SHE UNMASKS HER INNER MAGIC

By Hydee Hall

I spent a great deal of time alone as a child. I had no brothers or sisters growing up, and I was a latchkey kid with two parents who worked very long hours. Yet I always "felt" I had something around me. I knew I was not alone, and it was this feeling that gave me the comfort and love that I needed throughout my life to survive. I was born depressed, hungry for joy, and looking for a way not to drown in pain.

During especially difficult times, I would go outside, look at the trees, and feel their presence in my heart. Like magic, I would feel the company of "something" letting me know it was okay and I was not alone. It also helped immensely to have a pet dog. Her devoted presence soothed me as she listened to my words *and* my silence. She was not only my best friend, but the only one in my life who gave me unconditional love.

Throughout my teens, twenties, and thirties, I learned that it was far easier to hide my depression by wearing a mask and playing a part. My depression often felt like a can of paint above my head, with the paint in slow motion spilling all over me. I could then protect myself and choose to be anybody I needed to be. I could completely detach myself, and be outside myself, essentially watching myself play the part I had strategically chosen for that day. This was my coping mechanism, my safe way to participate in life. Being a typical Virgo, I excelled at taking on the characteristics of each of my masks. They not only gave me the ability to be creative and "be" anyone I wanted to be, but, more importantly, hide and protect the real me.

It was finally in my forties that I hit a desperate moment of exhaustion. I yelled out that I could no longer continue my life the way it was. At that moment, I surrendered. I experienced a gut-wrenching cry that came from a place I had no idea existed. I was finally ready to give up the way I was living. *I needed help.*

I will never forget the date. On April 1st, 2008, a "Spirit On Site" (or what I like to call an *SOS*) came through for me for the first time. The SOS had a sense of humor, proven by choosing to appear on April Fool's Day! It was a turning point in my life that forced me to look at a number of things within myself while an army of spiritual gurus made their presence known each step of the way. All of a sudden, there were messages and directions along the way— so many "coincidences"—as people were placed right in front of me to teach me and guide me forward.

The first priority at hand was shedding the FEAR that had been ingrained in me from the time I was created in my mother's womb. I had no idea that in shedding that fear it would be the inception of immense GRATITUDE. How was it possible that I had lived a life for so long in fear?

As I shed the layers and layers of fear, living became

more vibrant. I was seeing things as if it were for the first time and everything was brighter. This incredible pivotal point in my forties was truly an amazing gift from the Universe. I also felt a huge responsibility in receiving this gift, and proceeded carefully as I inherently knew at some point I would need to share my story and be of service to other beautiful souls. That little girl who hardly ever spoke or expressed any emotions was coming out at the midpoint of her life here on earth and she was going to be AUTHENTIC for the first time ever.

Next came FORGIVENESS. I had to learn to forgive myself for wearing all those masks and hiding that little girl. Getting in touch with my inner child was an amazing emotional experience, kind of like meeting an interesting stranger who seems very familiar. At one point on my spiritual journey, I felt like I gave birth to her. I had a very vivid dream (and rarely do I remember my dreams) where on this particular night I saw myself in hard labor, giving birth to this lovely, sweet, innocent spirit. As with my three sons, I immediately fell in love with this baby the moment I saw her. She was exquisitely beautiful and I embraced her with every fiber of my being. I knew precisely upon giving birth to her that I would love myself unconditionally and never ever again focus on my flaws.

At last, COMPASSION flowed freely from my inner core to my inner child. I saw her big smile for the first time in my mind. I saw her warm brown eyes and how bright and beautiful they were. Her messy hair was soft to the touch and I marveled at the lively curls that went in all different directions. All the hateful words that she had heard as a child meant nothing anymore. I really felt her for the first time ever and she was finally being fed LOVE. I was overcome with intense affection for her. She was so charming, so lively, and spirited! I embraced her, really hugged her and kissed her like no one had ever done when I was little. The connection was intense and purely magical. Life dramatically changed.

I was then on an adventure to intimately know that little girl. There were so many layers to this knowing and the process had its moments where I briefly questioned myself, but there's a reason for every step. I have learned to TRUST. I trust myself. I trust the Universe. I trust my SOS team.

I am grateful, blessed, and in awe of taking the chance at this stage of my life to have the COURAGE to make a difference in my future. There is no going back to the way I lived before as I have sipped, tasted, and consumed this magical knowingness. I cherish every gift, every revelation, and every "coincidence" that shows up. Sometimes it takes a leap of faith to take that first baby step and then two big steps back come next. Trust the pace. Everything gets revealed at precisely the moment it should.

I devote time and energy every day to my spirituality. Some days it is just a couple of minutes where it is as simple as a prayer of gratitude; other days I give myself several hours. I find my connections to spirit just by being mindful and observant in everything I do, whether it's gardening or washing the dishes. I have days where I seek haven in my special Goddess room (aka Female Nourishment Cave) and it is there where I read, reflect, and cherish who I am, what my soul is, and my deep connection to Source.

Looking back on it all, uncovering my inner magic could not have happened without the collapse of the person wearing the mask. It is in that heart wrenching pain of surrendering where my life prepared me for the birth of that little girl to emerge and be one with ME. She is ingrained in every fiber of my being and reminds me that I am always connected to SPIRIT.

This magical connection at times overwhelms me with tears of intense bliss and immense joy. It is in this magic, where there is unlimited forgiveness, compassion, authenticity, courage, love and trust.

SHE BEGINS HEARING HER SOUL

By Isabella Aponte

I attended an all-girls Catholic High School in Philadelphia. We wore maroon jumpsuits that were forbidden to rise above the knee. My mom is a devout Catholic with a large portrait of the Virgin Mary hanging in our dining room; crosses hung above every door. My father's mentor and role model was a Catholic priest. Not only did I have to confess my sins to Father George on a weekly basis, but I was also scolded if I ever missed church or even showed up late. I was not given any option on what to believe or how to live my life, other than the teachings of the Catholic Church; it was the religion of my family, and therefore my religion, as well.

Even after spending eight years at a Catholic elementary school, I still had so many unanswered questions. What if I wasn't sure what I believed exactly? Why were my doubts met with reprimands as opposed to information? I remember going home after an especially hard day in religion class and telling my parents that I was unsure if I really wanted to be a

Catholic. While they were extremely disappointed, they were more baffled than anything. They never expected me or my sisters to question their lifelong beliefs. What I really wanted was just to have options in what I learned about life, options about what I believed, and options on how I lived my life.

The summer after my senior year of high school, I counted down the days until I could move to New York City and begin my freshman year of college. I had decided that there was no other place for me than New York. I had visited the city often, and fell in love with the enormous buildings, the unforgettable skyline, and the massive amounts of people moving quickly through the streets. Every part of Manhattan made it seem as if it were a place people came to live out their dreams.

I had it all planned out: I would quickly immerse myself into the "New York City life" and live out my dream of becoming a writer. However, when I finally moved there, all of the things I loved about New York quickly blurred into the background as I felt everything about myself changing. The enormous buildings suddenly made me feel much smaller. The skyline seemed to become the symbol of an intangible dream. So many people made me feel extremely lonely. I felt as if New York had failed me. There was too much change all at once for my 18-year-old self to handle. But what I did not realize was that I was just truly beginning to unearth a part of me I never knew existed.

Through all of this confusion, I threw myself into my favorite courses in college, which were English and to my surprise, religion. This was my first experience of religion being presented in an objective way. It was not shoved down my throat, and I was not forced to blindly believe anything. Learning about all the different religions and beliefs of the world really began to open my mind. I actually wanted to invest time in what I believed in and figure out how my beliefs could affect my way of life. I visited churches, synagogues, Buddhist temples, religious exhibits, and much more just to learn about the different ways of experiencing life.

As one part of my dream seemed to be falling apart, who I was and what I believed began to be pieced together. This was the very first time that my eyes were opened to the fact that I had control over who I wanted to be and how I lived my life. It was not until college that I began to learn about all the ways that I could become a more aware human being.

Gaining the knowledge of all these different beliefs and each religion's perspective of the soul is what opened me up to my own soul's journey. I spent many nights on my twin sized bed, up on the top bunk in my small dorm room that I shared with four girls, reflecting on everything I had been learning, while debating whether or not to return home. There was this feeling in the pit of my stomach telling me that after just three months in New York City, it was okay to go home; *just do what will make you happy*. In some small way, I knew that this "pit" was not just a gut feeling; there was something inside me that I needed to become more aware of, to care for, and to listen to.

After returning home to Philadelphia, I felt as if I was starting from square one. I applied to Temple University where I could commute to and from school. Since I was spending so much time at home, I also began to explore my changing neighborhood. My once small, residential neighborhood was becoming a booming business area with a new store or restaurant popping up almost every week. In the midst of all this neighborhood change, one of my favorite shops was still there: The Little Candy Shoppe.

I vividly remember entering the small shop for the first time in the summer of 2010: bright pink walls, vintage mirrors, and every candy you could imagine was on display in glass cases. The smell of chocolate would linger the entire time you were in the Shoppe.

Of all these enticing qualities, Hayley, the owner, was what stood out the most to me. My first impression of her was that I had never met someone quite as inviting and charming as she was. Her beautiful long, black hair and bright smile already made her stand out, but it was truly her personality that drew me, along with many other customers, back to the store.

I visited the store often and grew extremely connected to Hayley. Every time I stopped by, I would silently hope it was a slow day so that she and I could just talk. Hayley would tell me about her life, and although she was only 24 years old, it had seemed as if she had already lived so many lives. She had been through numerous trials and tribulations, yet she was truly one of the most optimistic and selfless people I had ever met. One of her finest qualities was being a great listener. I must selfishly admit that most days it was her listening to me, my stories, and the struggles I was facing in my life. Not only did she listen, but she would offer advice and sometimes, when needed, just a hug. She knew exactly how to respond.

After leaving New York, I felt as if my spiritual journey had become stagnant and I needed a new way to satiate my soul's curiosity. Hayley was the one who helped me take the next big leap to continue my education which helped me reconnect with my soul. She offered advice on matters she had dealt with in her own life that would help me recognize the overwhelming feeling in the pit of my stomach I continued to endure. She guided me to read books, such as *Siddhartha, The Alchemist,* and *The Secret,* that allowed my brain to understand my gut feelings. These titles helped me make sense of my search for "more", as well as gain a better sense of self and consciousness. I became sure that these feelings and my thirst to learn other ways of living were both the voice of my soul. I could now identify it—and I was listening.

The more I learned, the more I wanted to know about the self, the soul, and consciousness. I wanted to become my own guide and started to do my own work. I began to take care of my soul through unapologetically listening and making decisions based on what was best for me, my gut, and my feelings. This is the path I am still on.

A pivotal moment came when I was able to share my journey with my younger sister. She had been undergoing her own personal passages, which had taken her to more places than the average 20-year-old may experience. She continuously inspires me to carry on with my own path just by vivaciously and fearlessly living out her own. Being able to have someone to share, relate, and turn to has urged me to share my story with others.

My journey of the soul is truly just beginning. There are still many times when I am tempted to ignore my soul's yearnings because what it longs for is scary or not "in my plan." However, I take myself back to when I was sitting on that top bunk when I made the decision that altered my complete sense of self and my beliefs: choosing to leave New York and return to Philly honored my quest to listen and connect with my soul. I have come to realize that my discovery of the soul was a domino effect of choices.

Sometimes we continue to wait and look for these huge lightning-striking moments to make a change in our lives, without even realizing that it can be the small talks with a friend or reading a few soul-searching books that can unfold a transformative and culminating process of greater self-realization.

SHE AWAKENS TO HER SOUL'S TALENTS

By Lorraine Paul

If you had told me that two well-groomed eyebrows would lead to the final realization that my marriage of 19 years was over, I would have thought you were absolutely nuts. But as I sat at dinner with my husband, the waiter standing at our table had the most incredible eyebrows—and I could hear his thoughts.

The waiter: "I shouldn't have waxed my eyebrows. They look too perfect."

Then I impulsively responded out loud, "Not at all, they suit you!"

He looked at me and smiled. We continued discussing his eyebrows, coming to the conclusion that if he were in New York City no one would think twice about how they looked, but instead, we were in very blue collar Whitestone, Queens. We laughed and he went back to attend to his tables.

My husband then turned to me, dismay and confusion on his face. "He didn't say anything to you! Why did you start talking about the guy's eyebrows?"

I was surprised. "Yes, he did! He clearly said he shouldn't have waxed his eyebrows and I tried to reassure him. I'm not exactly sure what's wrong with that!"

"You're crazy!" My husband looked away, shaking his head in disgust at me.

I realized I had heard the waiter telepathically, yet the waiter didn't look at me like I was crazy. More unsettling to me though, was that my husband and I were on opposite sides of the table on an issue yet again. I made it through the rest of that meal with a soft veil of tears that came from years of hurt and humiliation. I decided then and there that I would not suffer through any more years of heartache, scorn, and disrespect with this man.

I had opened up to more of my spiritual path and soul gifts in recent years, and as I did, my husband had grown more agitated and hurtful. I had always been involved in the local church, which he tolerated, but now that I was learning about the angelic realm, he had zero interest in hearing about *that* crazy topic. I knew in my heart that my husband and I were growing farther apart. I began to practice yoga and meditate, he took a job at a gun range; I yearned for peace and harmony, he got more involved with mixed martial arts and became increasingly aggressive.

Thinking about divorce brought up my own childhood challenges of growing up in a broken home. After my parents' divorce, my father didn't contribute financially, yet he did offer an overabundance of emotional damage. My mother did the best she could, but it was extremely hard to make ends meet as a single working woman. As a result, my childhood had planted two very significant seeds in my psyche: maintaining tranquility and achieving financial stability were both essential. My husband's childhood story was similar. We both felt our parents' needs took precedence over our needs when we were growing up. The "Free to be YOU and ME" mantra of the 1970's pertained to them, the adults, not the dependent children. My husband and I were two broken people who thought we understood each other because of our similar upbringings and we never wanted to perpetuate this unhealthy cycle. Too bad we didn't know that two broken people don't equal one completely healthy relationship.

My standard way of dealing with challenges in our relationship was to address it once and hope for change. To maintain the all-important tranquility, I'd ignore it if nothing changed and then just pray the issue would eventually resolve itself. My certified "ostrich approach" to difficult situations had never worked well in the past, and I'd soon discover it definitely wasn't going to work now.

The month following that telepathic dinner, my eight-year-old daughter and I spent the last week of June on Fire Island where my mother had a summer place. We rented a small house nearby and, as usual, my husband was too busy to join us for the entire time. When he finally arrived, he took my daughter out for dinner. I was happy to have a break, so I went out with my mother and her friends. I was having a good time, when one of my mother's friends turned to me and said, "You have such sadness in your eyes!" I had no idea what he was talking about.

As our conversation continued throughout the evening, I finally realized he was right. Not only was I terribly unhappy, I wasn't even living; I was just surviving. I had become one of the walking dead, just going through the motions. My life was a complete façade. The saddest part of this realization was the fact that the only one I had convinced I was happy was me. Since I never saw my mom's friend again, I also realized that my angels were definitely communicating with me through him that night.

To be completely honest, I struggled to remain centered and love-based during my ensuing divorce. However, my ex apparently did not get the Conscious Uncoupling memo I had sent out into the Universe. I vowed to get through this whole process consciously and with intention. Since I now knew I was surrounded by angels, I also knew that I deserved to be happy.

I credit my aunt with opening me up to different ways of understanding life from a spiritual perspective. Being in her presence was like coming home to the smell of Toll House cookies; that feeling of warmth and comfort just radiated from her. One time she informed me that she could communicate with her crystal. She removed the Herkimer diamond necklace she was wearing, held it in front of her, and proceeded to ask it questions. The shiny little diamond would swing side to side for "no" and back and forth for "yes." I knew that she loved to visit a trusted local psychic who communicated with departed loved ones, but I wasn't quite sure what to make of this crystal communication thing. The way it happily responded "yes" or "no" to her various questions was so bizarre to me at first.

My aunt eventually recommended that I read Michael Newton's book, *Journey of Souls, Case Studies of Life between Lives*. I believed in God and the afterlife, but I had never really given reincarnation much thought. It turned out this book really opened my eyes to new possibilities and even deeper questions.

I also found someone in New York City who specialized in past life regression and I booked a session. During this period, I became aware of seeing repeating numbers everywhere, especially 11:11. I discovered Doreen Virtue's *Angel Numbers 101* and began to understand the meaning of these numbers. I then read every book she had ever written over the next few weeks. It was extremely comforting to imagine that we are actually surrounded by angels who are not only willing, but available 24/7 to assist us in absolutely anything we need help with. Before reading her book, I had just relied on my old standby, Archangel Michael. Now I realized I had my own personal team of angels!

My spiritual seeking then led me to Reiki healing. My cat had been diagnosed with liver failure, so I decided to take an Animal Reiki class to assist her in whatever way I could. Through the classes I took, from Beginner to the Master Level, I met some wonderful people I would have never met in my "regular" life: some communicated with animals, some worked with crystals, and all had interesting ideas regarding the way in which we maneuver through this life. I began each day with the basic Reiki precepts: For today only, do not anger, do not worry, be humble, be honest in your work, be compassionate to yourself and others. These principals helped me focus on today and not get too caught up in worrying about the future.

Unexpectedly, the most challenging time of my life turned out to be the most uplifting. As the divorce and life situations became increasingly difficult, I'd find new books, blogs, and teachers. I would receive immense comfort from a variety of spiritual readings. During one of these readings, a woman who knew nothing about me informed me that Mother Mary would like to be invited to assist me during my Reiki sessions. Mother Mary wanted me to consider her as a sister, and she would be right behind my left shoulder. Sure, I'll consider Mother Mary, who is standing behind me, as my sister—who wouldn't?

I was alone for the first time in my life, and yet I found myself surrounded by loving people offering more love than I could ever have imagined. Unlike having to take the time to read mainstream self-help books, my newfound teachers and mentors were always available to me. I could connect with them through email or Facebook and they'd be there, willing to offer support, advice, and counsel.

I recall I was very apprehensive about filing a motion in family court during the divorce proceedings, so I posted something vague on Facebook asking for prayers. The next day, my astrologer sent me an email. She had looked up my astrology reading for the day and assured me all would be well. She wrote, "Wherever you find yourself, imagine Archangel Michael literally standing right there saying, 'I've got your back, sister.' This is an opportunity for you to trust more, knowing that as a Divine Child of the Universe you are being taken care of as you move through these energies and complete what you are done with."

It was amazing to know that not only did Mother Mary consider me a sister, but now Archangel Michael did, too! At one point in my life, this would have sounded crazy to me, but I sure preferred my new reality to my old one.

The divorce is now final, I have full custody of my daughter, and we have since manifested a beautiful home on the water, surrounded by wonderful new friends. And when I say "we," I mean my daughter and me. Together, we made a dream board, and YES, they do work! As we go through our day, we ask the angels to send us a little sign, like feathers or butterflies, and then count how many we encounter. I am so very grateful every day. I can finally breathe! I've done the spiritual work!

Then I realized, uh…not quite.

Through all the shifts and a-ha moments, I still could not forgive my ex-husband. I searched for books on forgiveness. I read unbelievable stories of people forgiving much worse situations than I'd experienced, but to no avail. At one point I tried to look at it from another perspective.

Numerology presented the idea that not only did I, as a soul, plan this lifetime, but all the current people in my life chose to be here as supporting characters in my soul story. If I chose this life, then I'm no longer a victim. I chose this man to assist me in my soul's evolution. Then I'd think, "Why was I crazy enough to have chosen this man and this life?" But since thoughts are energy, I realized that if I couldn't forgive him right now, I could at least begin to forgive myself. *Get back on track, sister!* This spiritual path can require fortitude.

Eventually, my memories of my marriage began to lose their harshness. I truly do believe that my ex-husband did the best he could with the tools available to him. You can only offer to others what you have to give and nothing more. He agreed to this role during our life between lives with the intention of profound love for me. Because I believe that, then there's nothing to forgive.

My new life is going extremely well because of all of the spiritual tools that still support my growth. My daily Reiki practice helps me remain grounded. I have a lovely collection of crystals which I now include in my Reiki sessions. And the belief in our souls planning our life between lives means nothing is being "done to me." I'm not a victim. That is such a source of empowerment to me.

Feeling more empowered helped me trust my telepathic messages more on a daily basis. Offering Reiki to our furry friends led to animal communication, and then receiving messages from departed loved ones. Angel Card Readings have spurred even more conversations with the angelic realm. Every day brings something fascinating.

And I now realize that the angels sometimes use something quite unexpected—like telepathy with a waiter!—to show you a better way; a new way of moving in your world. For me, it was a pair of well-groomed eyebrows that began the process of deeper spiritual awareness and choosing another path that was empowering—and certainly never boring. By letting go of what no longer serves you, you can open up more room for creating a life beyond your wildest dreams.

SHE EMBRACES THE GIFT OF THE DEER

By Connie Cole

Astring of abusive relationships had left me shattered; low self-esteem and negative self-talk had been my companions for many years. Although participation in a spiritual community had helped alleviate much of the negativity, the same old issues lingered under the surface.

One late spring day, I felt abandoned by my friends who had all gone to upstate New York for a special community event. I was quite resentful that I was alone here in Austin, while they were all together having fun at a big party. I was plagued with thoughts of anxiety, uncertainty, and insecurity, thoughts that kept repeating non-stop in my head, creating a vortex leading to rejection. It made no difference that the decision to stay in Austin had been mine. Traveling to New York and unpaid time off did not fit my self-concept of a fiscally responsible adult. No frivolous spending for me! Frustrated with the whole situation, I continued to criticize myself.

After moping around the house and spending way too much time in that negative head space, I decided to go for a drive. The least I could do for myself was to enjoy the beauty of Austin's hills on this sunny day. I felt drawn to drive on Bee Cave Road, to enjoy its winding curves and the beautiful scenery of the Texas hill country; to feel connected to the land and the beauty of the earth.

As I drove, I noticed along the road that a deer had been hit by a car and apparently had died quite recently. I acknowledged its presence with a small prayer and kept driving.

Suddenly, I heard a Voice say, "Go back and pick up that deer."

What the heck, I thought. *I would never pick up a dead animal.* I ignored the Voice and kept on driving. A few minutes later, the Voice again said, "Go back and pick up that deer."

I didn't know what to think about this. First, I was hearing a voice—not a normal occurrence for me—and secondly, it's telling me to do something that I've never done before and really had no intention of doing now. But I made a U-turn and drove back past the deer—not stopping.

For a third time, I heard the Voice direct me. "Go back and pick up that deer."

Another U-turn. This time I stopped. The entire situation felt very strange and otherworldly. I opened the back of my vehicle and decided to put the deer in it. I had never picked up a dead animal before, and was finding it to be almost impossible to move the deer, much less pick it up. Then a truck pulled to the side of the road in front of my car, a man got out, and walked around to the back where I was standing near the deer.

He seemed to understand my dilemma, and wordlessly, he gently picked up the deer and placed it on a blanket in the back of my vehicle. I looked at him and thanked him. No other words were spoken. He just walked back to his truck and drove away.

I had moved completely out of normal space and time. Now I had a dead deer on a blanket in the back of my car. *What the heck was I supposed to do now?*

I felt drawn to drive a few miles to some land where I had participated in a community event a few weeks before. Once there, I was attracted to an obscure spot under the trees that seemed like a nurturing space that a deer might enjoy. I awkwardly and slowly maneuvered the heavy deer from the car to the womblike space, unsure of where my strength came from. It was bewildering to be doing all of this, yet it seemed as though I received direct guidance about each next action to take.

I remembered that I kept a small Buck knife in my glove compartment, so I grabbed it. Knowing absolutely nothing about skinning an animal, I felt guided to cut from under the neck straight down the body to the pelvic area. Praying as I worked, I slowly and gently removed the entire deer skin using the 2-1/2" blade.

I was completely stunned to find that the deer was pregnant—a tiny fawn was inside her. Tears flowed quickly and without restraint as I thought of the two lives that were lost. My heart was breaking for the doe, for the fawn, for my faltering relationship with my son, and for the babies I had lost myself—the lives that, like the fawn, had not had the opportunity to be born. I was awestruck at the realization of the significance and connectedness of all life in all its many beautiful forms.

I had no idea what to do with the doe's body, but it

felt appropriate to say prayers to the spirits of the directions and the spirits of the land, thanking them for the gift I had received and asking that they accept the gift of this doe as an offering of food to other animals or insects.

Exhausted, I returned to my car with the blanket and deer skin. I had skinned a deer in the woods with a Buck knife. The improbability of this whole experience was beginning to sink in. I was amazed that I had been guided to the deer; that I had allowed myself to open up enough to trust the guidance that I had received, and to fully accept the gift of two animal lives that had been bestowed on me.

Then I was left with the question of how to process a deer hide. I had absolutely no idea how to do this. None whatsoever. Still inhabiting an otherworldly realm, I drove to the library to find out how to tan the hide. I forgot that I had blood on my hands and that I must smell of deer. I cleaned up the best I could in the ladies room before entering the quiet space. The first book I touched was exactly what I needed.

Heading home from the library, I stopped at a feed store I had not noticed before. As a modern woman defined by her urban environment, looking for taxidermy tools and knowledge was quite surreal. The feed store was part of an agricultural culture that was totally unfamiliar to me, but I bought the recommended tools, lime and a scraping tool, before returning home.

Still transported to an altered space and time, I put the deer hide in a soaking bath as described in the instructions and began scraping all the hair from the coat, carefully tanning the deer hide. I was then drawn outside to a nearby open lot where I found a perfect branch of willow. Magic seemed to be occurring at every step! I fashioned a hoop from the willow, ultimately stretching the deer skin over the hoop to create a shield. As I worked, the Voice once again directed me to use leather strips to tie the deer hide to the willow hoop to dry.

Natural spots that began to appear near the center of the hide as it dried reminded me of a jaguar. In one of my recent dreams, a female jaguar was lovingly playing with her cubs until an unusual sound brought her to full alert, transforming her into an expert hunter ready to pounce on anything or anyone that threatened her young.

The shield began calling me to decorate it with meaningful symbols. Again, I doubted my ability as I had never been trained as an artist. The call was strong, though, and I began to paint symbols from recent dreams and visions in each quadrant of the shield.

The east quadrant represented new beginnings, new ideas, the initiation of new projects, and in that quadrant, I painted a phoenix, rising from flames to experience its rebirth.

The south quadrant represented the growth of ideas, and relationships and connections with others. There I painted a spirit being with a butterfly on each arm. It was apparent to me that the butterflies represented individuals whose relationships were created through connection with the spirit.

The west quadrant represented one's inner reflections, spiritual guidance, and connection with the spirit. There I added the spiral symbol reminding me of my inner evolving journey, as well as the thunderbird that represented not only the thunder beings that bring awareness through shock and awe, but that served as spiritual guides.

The north quadrant represented completion of a journey and the wisdom gained from that journey. The symbols that appeared there were an eagle roosting in a tree, a lizard walking toward the north, and snakes emerging from eggs. Each of these symbols had previously appeared in my dreams, and each imparted spiritual medicine for healing and transformation.

The upward and downward directions were represented by Grandfather Sky and Grandmother Earth. At the very center of the shield I painted a large gong, a golden yellow like the sun, representing movement beyond the world of understanding, movement toward the Great Mystery.

For some reason, I felt a request to add a long braid of my hair to the shield. I had saved a long ponytail from a previous haircut, and I braided it to add to the shield. This long braid had appeared in a dream as the method by which I would be pulled into heaven. As I added the symbols and other items, the shield attained greater significance as a personal symbol of strength and protection. I was elated with the completed shield and proud of my accomplishment. It felt like a depiction of my inner self and my unique journey. I placed the shield on my bedroom wall, where it continually radiates meaning to me on many different levels.

A couple of weeks after completing the shield, I again felt that I was specifically summoned to the same obscure spot under the trees where I had buried the deer and that had felt so nurturing to me on my earlier visit. There, where I had left the deer and the fawn surrounded by prayers, nothing remained of the deer except her four hooves. I also saw a small eagle feather exactly where the deer had lain. I was overcome by emotion. The gifts of the hooves and feather seemed to honor me for being still and listening, for following Spirit's guidance, and for accomplishing the given tasks with humility and a gentle heart. I joyfully accepted these gifts from the animals.

I kept the hooves in a special wooden container lined with fragrant herbs, and I wrapped the quill of the eagle feather with thick red thread so that I could attach it to the shield. A Voice within led me to add it to the western quadrant near the spiral and the thunderbird, to remind me always of my connection to spirit. I believe these gifts are a physical manifestation of my connection to all life.

These days, the shield holds a prominent place on my living room wall. It is a constant reminder of what I learned following the Voice within and how being willing to quiet the incessant internal negative litany allowed me to open my heart enough to find a way to nurture myself. This heart opening offered an opportunity to experience the possibilities inherent in the present moment, even when they seem as outlandish as picking up a dead deer.

Throughout my time with the deer, I chose to listen to the guidance that was offered, to trust what I was hearing, and to be courageous enough to take action based on that guidance. I was especially grateful that I had stayed with the experience through completion, despite my discomfort with the process.

When we are willing to surrender to infinite possibility, we open to embracing precious spiritual gifts, like my astonishing gift of the deer.

SHE TAKES STEPS INTO HER INNER SELF

By Debora Kiyono

"This is not what we agreed. You are not honoring your word."

I spoke in a very calm, firm and strong voice to Emi. These words were not part of the speech I had in mind. However, they were effective; she heard me.

I had gone over to Emi's place in order to say in person what I had already texted her: that I didn't have the time to do what she was asking, that I wasn't obliged to do things for her, and that she was not respecting me. But again, she just ignored what I said. She insisted that I was the only one who could help her because I was single and had no kids. It made me really angry that she thought that I did not have anything else to do but be at her service. I was about to lose control when my Inner Self, the deeper part of me that was paying attention to what was going on, saw the great opportunity to take over. That's when those spontaneous words came out: "You are not honoring your word."

Unknowingly, I had said the magic words. For a few seconds there was silence in the room. Emi's eyes were wide in astonishment. All of a sudden, the discussion turned in a different direction and took on a different tone.

"You're right. We agreed that we were not going to do this," she said, defeated.

I walked out of her door and felt like I had walked through a portal into a different world. It was the end of a story that had begun long ago. As I saw the scenes of a past life coming and going, I understood that we both had fulfilled our parts in our soul agreement. She had insisted until she pushed me to the edge. And because of that, she gave me the best gift ever: the opportunity to bring out the force from within me. I was immensely grateful to her. Our contract was over. We were each set free.

When I calmed down after our exchange, I wanted to know more about this inner force. I felt it was a new beginning for my story.

"How do you get to know someone better?" I wondered.

"We go out on dates," I heard my Inner Self answer.

It seemed very illogical to date myself, I thought. But I had this burning desire to know my Inner Self better.

"What would you like to do on our first date?" I imagined I was talking on the phone to myself, and waited for a reply.

It did not take long to find an answer. A friend had told me about a photography exhibit in town. My heart smiled wide and I knew that it was the answer. And the surprises did not stop there. The exhibit's title was "Genesis." As I walked through the exhibit, appreciating all the photographs taken in places where modern civilization had not yet had an impact, I was talking to myself:

"Look, what a beautiful place! I would like to visit it someday."

And "Oh, my God, it seems that he captured this person's soul! It's amazing!"

And "How close do you think he was from this elephant in order to take this shot?"

And there were many more comments as if I was admiring the photographs with a friend. When I least expected it, I realized what my Inner Self was trying to tell me: "We are on a journey to get to know our origins, our Genesis, who we are in essence."

I was in awe. It was the best date ever! I wondered why I did not have this idea before. I knew my tank of love was filled after that quality time.

As the dates continued, the communication between us opened up. My Inner Self and I became very creative. Most of the dates were art related: movies, exhibits, theater, concerts; classical, contemporary, kids. The only rule was it had to be adventurous and fun.

While visiting a Salvador Dali exhibit, a lady stopped and spoke to me. "Hello! You may like this upcoming dance performance because you are Japanese. Are you Japanese?" She was one of those people who could talk for hours. She did not give me a chance to answer any of her questions. She handed me the program brochure.

While she continued to talk, I read the description of the contemporary dance performance that she had pointed out to me. I realized how much I was craving to watch a performance like this.

"Where do I get a ticket for this show?" I asked her. She smiled. She had accomplished her mission and did not mind that I gave no attention to the other things she had said. She gave me directions to the theatre and joyfully said farewell.

On the day of the performance, I was overwhelmed by a strange, uncomfortable feeling growing inside of me; it was making me feel very anxious.

"What is this feeling?" I asked myself.

"It's called fear." Me, afraid? No way!

"Fear of what?"

I was surprised by the answer. "Fear of going out alone in the evening. You think it's not safe for a woman to walk alone at night. Fear of what people will think about you: a woman alone in the night is a slut."

"Honestly? Do I think like that? It does not sound like me at all." I insisted stubbornly.

"Check again." It was the last word.

As I was getting prepared to leave for the show, I could feel the fear growing stronger. I had no option but to pay attention to it. As I walked to the car, I was scared to death. Yet I would not give up; I would not allow fear to defeat me. It was about time to face it. As I moved toward the car, I saw clearly that those fears did not belong to me, that they had been implanted in me and that they were trying to stay with me. I kept going, alone out in the night, and yet feeling braver and more powerful with each passing moment. By the time I arrived at the theatre, the fears were all gone and the show turned out to be fantastic.

Another time, a six-year-old girl came up to me and asked, "Do you see colors in people?" She inquired as if it was the most natural thing to ask a stranger.

"No, do you?" I smiled. She nodded yes.

"What color am I now?" I asked. I was curious, although I already knew the answer.

"Pink," she said, sounding like she was having a

very good time with this conversation.

"Do you actually believe she is right?" her dad asked, surprised and skeptical as he approached us.

"She has a very high sense of clairvoyance. I have the sense of claircognizance and clairsentience. That's how I know what she is talking about." I replied.

He did not say a word. But I could see clearly the "Uh—Clair… What?" expression on his face. It was funny. I began to have a good time with this unexpected encounter.

"Clairvoyance means clear seeing. This is possible when we use and develop our extrasensory perception. I believe that when she sees the colors, she is not looking with her physical eyes. What she sees is called an aura." The girl smiled in approval.

"Claircognizance is clear knowing and clairsentience is clear feeling," I continued. "Claircognizants just know. They don't know how, the knowledge just jumps out. Clairsentients feel thoughts, feelings, and vibrations from other people, things, and places. It depends on how they develop this perception."

I went on talking about all I knew about extrasensory perception gifts. I was secretly surprised to hear myself giving these explanation to the father. I wanted to ask my Inner Self if it had known that I had these gifts all the time since I was just now becoming aware of them.

"Do I have this thing, too?" he asked, clearly afraid of the answer he already knew.

"Yes," I said.

"Which one?" he asked, wanting some confirmation. "You know." I smiled, waved to both of them, and walked away.

When I was alone I laughed because I remembered how I hated it when somebody gave me this kind of answer during my unconscious days. Of course I knew the answer, but I wanted someone to tell me, instead of trusting my inner knowing. He probably didn't like me that day. It did not matter. One day he will be laughing with a similar reaction.

My spiritual awakening was unexpected and had a series of interesting events. The incident with Emi was a beginning point for me on my spiritual journey as it initiated a series of experiences when my inner force emerged. Then my desire to know my Inner Self more made the world bigger, more interesting, and more loving. I woke up. I became more aware of myself, my feelings, my thoughts, and my gifts. I became conscious of the infinite possibilities available in the Universe. I now know that there is no turning back. And I am so grateful for that!

SHE REWRITES HER LIFE WITH HO'OPONOPONO

By Teresa Leming

Another night of "The Crying Game." Not the 1992 box office hit; more like a pathetic after-school special called, "Her Puffy Eyes." Other titles of my relationship films could be "It's All His Fault" and "He Did It To Me." The leading men who were cast in these gut-wrenching dramas would include my absent biological father; my overly strict, abusive step-father; my first boyfriend; my first unfaithful husband; the random men between husband number one and sexually confused husband number two; and then a couple of major disappointments after that.

The heroine of every one of these blockbusters was me: Teresa the Crazy, an irrational, obsessive and an overly insecure woman that progressively mastered self-desecration. And the predictable finale of each one of these encounters included explosions, dramatics, and emotional hysterics (3D glasses included at no extra charge).

Even as the leading male role changed, I stuck with the same ending of being the victim. If I continued to blame "him," then I did not have to acknowledge my own role in the ongoing drama. Thankfully I had a huge breakthrough in 2009 around my relationship patterns that led me to change my unconscious habits and heal deeply with profound gratitude.

But before we fast-forward to the end of this story, let's rewind all the way back to 2006. I was still completely heartbroken and devastated two years after the demise of my second marriage, and felt that my only choice for happiness was to keep myself distracted with my career. At least that was a role I was good at performing.

As one of the top wholesale mortgage representatives in Las Vegas, Nevada, I lived the life that represented success. Before turning 40, I owned a big, beautiful home with a pool and luxury cars; indulged in lavish vacations; and had accrued plenty of money in the bank. I was proud of all of it—extremely proud. It wasn't bad for a girl who rose above her circumstances of being told she would never amount to anything in life, as well as an unexpected pregnancy at 15. Well, I had showed "him!"

But it became clearer that my life was also an illusion of bullshit.

In 2008, everything I had diligently acquired to prove myself a success was crumbling before my eyes. The special effects of my life were a giant façade as the stock market tanked. I had no real time to comprehend the magnitude of what was happening with the financial market: shock, fear, and denial rapidly became the constant emotions that consumed me. I watched my friends and colleagues lose their versions of success quickly, too. Big houses and expensive cars quickly exited, stage left. Before we knew it, the show was over — with no refunds.

Stumbling into 2009, one job after another came and went. I was hired by a bank only for it to close. Unfathomably, I held six or seven new jobs within a six-month period; a personal record I will never be comfortable breaking. My proudly accrued savings account suddenly went to making my monthly mortgage payment. I watched in horror as it became a hopeless, degrading, scary struggle, with "The End" eventually stamped on the home foreclosure papers. All was lost. I was homeless, jobless, and faced with two options: move in with my parents or move in with Mr. Dysfunctional. Can you guess which one I picked?

After I had had enough of living with the current "him," I actually began to realize that I had had enough of *me*. Nothing about me felt like *me*. I was no longer the motivated, confident, unstoppable woman I knew myself to be. I looked like crap because I felt like crap. Depressed, emotionally taxed, lost, and profoundly lonely. A part of me wanted to give up. I admit thoughts of washing down sleeping pills with a bottle of vodka played in my mind.

So I left. I packed up my Mercury Mariner with everything I could put inside it, and decided that sleeping in my car was far more appealing than another night with him. I drove with no intentions or destination. The highway and I were one for two days as I slowly realized I did have a target destination: my aunt's house in Texas. A judgment-free atmosphere awaited. Even better, complaining without responsibility was an Olympic sport in our family. Her house was where I needed to be as I would be welcomed with cocktails and free-range bitching.

After passing the Texas state line, I caught a glimpse of a Barnes & Noble sign off the freeway. I suddenly veered off the road and took the exit to the store. As if in a trance, I walked into the book store and went straight to the audio book section. I was instinctively drawn to the bottom shelf, where I grabbed *Zero Limits* by Dr. Joe Vitale and Dr. Ihaleakala Hew Len. I didn't have to even read the description, nor did I look at any other audio book options. I just bought it.

Back in the car, I listened intently to Joe Vitale tell the story of Dr. Hew Len and his experience of healing the criminally insane at Hawaii State Mental Hospital. AS every CD in the audio book played, my soul shifted more as I drove along the highway and cried away my own inner suffering. I felt angels with me for the first time ever. I could feel a change happening within me. At the moment, I didn't have a conscious comprehension of the changes. All I knew was that my heart was vibrating, my body was shaking, and my soul was melting like butter.

The simplicity of taking ownership for my life rocked my core. The silly little mantra of Ho'Oponopono: "I am sorry," "please forgive me," "thank you," and "I love you" played like heavenly intuitive music. I had such clarity hearing Joe's voice. Over and over, I finally saw how my leading men were the same *him*; a reoccurring scene that would keep playing until I looked within. Unstoppable tears poured down my cheeks.

I didn't get initially why it made sense, but intuitively, it did. Ho'Oponopono made perfect sense. Without hesitation, I repeated, "I am sorry; please forgive me, I love you." I said it for me! I felt instant compassion for the pain echoing in my inner child. The more I felt the words, the more I realized my role in creating my reality. Immediate love and tremendous peace soaked my heart. I knew I was not alone, and I was not unlovable.

I unexpectedly turned the car around somewhere in Texas and headed back to Vegas.

Within two weeks of my return, I had a new, respectable paying job with a title company working the foreclosure auction (go figure). I moved into an apartment that wasn't depressing and was sizable enough to take all my belongings out of storage. Those two positive developments ignited even more of my inner awakening. Countless mini-miracles then unfolded.

The Hawaiian healing technique quickly became my daily practice. For the first time, I wanted to understand my life's theme and purpose. Growing up, I had had a lot of religious conventionality. The God community I had lived in had unreasonable rules, embedded the fear of sin in my mind, was highly judgmental, and included some not-so-entertaining hypocrites. Nevertheless, "God" resonated in every aspect of this unique Hawaiian methodology, and my soul was yearning for more. I enrolled in my first Self-I-Dentity class as it was only a hop, skip, and a jump over to Milpitas, CA. I could not wait to meet the audio book's master instructor and mystical healer, Dr. Hew Len.

The Self-I-Dentity course was two days of information overload as I tried to comprehend the concept of aligning the Inner Family unit. The three roles of conscious mind, subconscious mind, and superconscious mind intrigued me. I believed in the importance of "care for the child," which is the subconscious mind. I grasped the possibility of programs and thought forms showing up in the physical world as our experiences. I thought it was cool that everything could involve the three parts of the mind and that everything might be alive.

The last couple of hours of the workshop weekend were comprised of testimonies. I sat in amazement listening to the results from other people's Ho'Oponopono *I Am Sorry* cleaning process. From Dr. Len, I learned how Ho'Oponopono teaches a new way of looking at ourselves and our lives. Our experiences will reoccur until we "clean" them. All problems will show up again and again. We have to forgive and repent for the transmutation of programs and thought forms.

Comprehending that EVERYTHING we experience is originating from our inner child (subconscious mind) through a replaying tape fascinated me. More so, it is a tape that has never healed from not only the current life, but also past lifetimes that originated from the beginning of your soul's experiences. The inner child can't help but recreate life experiences because the memory has never been released. It is essentially trapped on rewind.

I couldn't deny my results of this awakening experience. As I flipped through the Ho'Oponopono manuals, a feeling of peace and love consumed me. Inner knowing and desire were present. My soul craved the truth. I decided to accept and implement what made sense and disregard the rest.

Now eight years later, I am a rewritten heroine. My new role consists of the empowered qualities of ownership, gratitude, humbleness, and love. Slowly, Ho'Oponopono stripped away the old roles I had played. Now I take full ownership of my whole script. Nothing is done to me; it is done for me. I have sincere gratitude for each lesson presented. I am grateful for all the situations that befall me and for the souls who cross my path. I embrace a humble demeanor, as I want to see through the eyes of God. My commitment to treating everyone and everything with love boomerangs with love and peace. I am starting to feel hopeful for a new love story, too.

Ho'Oponopono is a spectacular clearing tool that effectively deletes lifetimes of pain and suffering. It took a while, but my neglected emotional world was finally safe to surface and heal the painful, traumatic memories that had been so deeply hidden within my unconscious role of victim.

"It's All His Fault" and "He Did It To Me" are no longer available in my life cinema. I am grateful to my previous leading men. Without them, I wouldn't have found myself or rediscovered a new superstar, God. Appreciation of my past now allows my present to be a new love story entitled, "Self-Healing".

Make no mistake: peace within is the ultimate happy ending.

SHE EMPOWERS

{ Owning Her Power }

"She knows it's time to make a change.
She feels it on an energetic level that she can't quite
describe and maybe doesn't even want to put into
words. It is a personal and sacred language, an inner
message between her and her Soul."

The Modern Heroine's Journey of Consciousness

SHE FINDS HER POWER BY
BEING FORCED INTO BATTLE

By Alison Baughman

Yes, people say mean things on social media and life is too short to argue with stupid people, but what I encountered in 2015 changed my mind about that. Nothing can prepare you for the day when you discover you are being crucified on social media and it is especially difficult when you are a public figure. When you have based your entire career on helping others and truly believe that you reap what you sow, you cannot help but be in disbelief that this is how the Universe rewards you.

Yes, I was mad at God that day and in the darkest days to follow.

My story begins by telling you that I am a successful professional Numerologist and have built a career spanning almost two decades. Honesty, integrity and dedication are of the utmost importance to me. I have done thousands of Numerology Readings, taught Numerology to hundreds of students, and worked hard to make the world aware of the insights Numerology has to offer. Yet being successful also made me a target. Even worse, I actually knew the person who was attacking me because he had heard of my work and asked for my insights on Numerology in the past.

At first, disparaging remarks directed at me came on Twitter. I tried to ignore them but the situation quickly escalated. This person had a tight-knit group of friends who joined in on the bullying, and before I knew it, I was being hit on multiple fronts. They sent derogatory messages about me to my followers on Twitter, created fake Twitter accounts to insult me, attacked my work and then attacked my looks, made up lies, and eventually came after my family.

The usual advice given for dealing with internet trolls is to ignore them, but that was impossible to do. If I blocked one account, another one would be created, so I was forced to deal with a daily stream of hateful insults. I was receiving spiteful emails, too, so it was becoming almost impossible to ignore.

I not only do spiritual work, but I live my life spiritually, so I decided to contact this bully to see if we could find a peaceful resolution. It was then that I realized I was not dealing with a rational person, but someone who was a special kind of crazy. He had a long history of going after other Numerologists so this was not his first time at the rodeo. It became clear that he had set the intention to "destroy me" and nothing I could say or do was going to change that. How did I know that? I received an email from him that quite literally said, "I will destroy you."

You can't accuse me of missing the obvious.

I was at the point where I thought it could not get any worse, but then I woke up one day to find that I had received 12 negative reviews on my recently published book in less than 24 hours. There was no question where the reviews came from because I recognized the names of his followers. They also chose to praise him by using his name in their reviews. My book was my pride and joy, and I had been experiencing great success with it. It was the highest rated book on Numerology on Amazon and was a best seller. The negative reviews quickly ended that. I do not think I have cried that hard in years. I felt so defeated. It was unfair, unjust, and downright cruel.

I was shaken to my very core. I always practice what I preach and I truly believe you reap what you have sown. I have supported and promoted countless people throughout my career; I have gone above and beyond for my clients; I poured my heart and soul into my Numerology practice; I always helped wherever I could—and THIS was my reward? My confidence was shattered, I was questioning my beliefs, and I honestly felt broken on every level.

Most importantly, I was angry at God and could not understand why this was happening. When I discovered my troll friend had created no fewer than three websites to try to redirect traffic from my website to a hateful page about me, I think I stopped talking to God for a few days.

Then God decided to answer me on Facebook.

Shortly after the negative Amazon reviews showed up, I posted about this experience on Facebook. I suppose you could call it having my own little pity party. I explained what happened and how devastated I was about the unjust attacks on my book. In short order, 165 amazing souls responded with an unprecedented show of support. Many wrote about how I had reached out and helped them in a time of need, describing acts of kindness I had long forgotten. Others told me how much my readings had influenced their lives in a positive way. My students chimed in, too, and when I read all of their wonderful, heart-warming posts, I began to realize I had been unaware of how many positive effects my work had had on people. I had just never given myself credit for it all.

I also became aware that God was letting me know that I had indeed reaped what I had sown. Shortly after that post, many people went to Amazon and left positive reviews for my book, which was so very kind of them. In the end, I realized perhaps all of this support was something I really needed to be shown and I thanked God for the lesson.

Despite this show of encouragement, the internet attacks continued and I was struggling with trying to ignore them. I spoke to a dear friend about what was going on and she could not understand why I would let someone so insignificant upset me so much. She asked a very pertinent question: "What does this guy represent to you?" and I was surprised by my answer. I found myself answering that he was my father, my brothers, my uncle, and every male figure in my childhood who had victimized me and caused me emotional pain.

I realized something else from that conversation. As a child, I had been helpless to fight back and here I was feeling victimized all over again. But now I was an adult and I could defend myself. However, I was still struggling with my spiritual beliefs about all this harassment. I knew the right thing to do was to take the high road, but it felt so wrong to me to sit back and allow the victimization to continue.

Taking the high road is not all it's cracked up to be.

One of the things I learned rather quickly is that you have little recourse against an internet bully. I learned by speaking to several lawyers that you could spend tens of thousands of dollars to try to legally prove defamation of character and end up having very little to show for it. I learned from the police that they are not the least bit interested in your case unless the person threatens you with physical harm. I learned from Twitter that, at the time, they had a very lax policy when it comes to harassment as almost everything falls under "freedom of speech." I also found out it takes an act of God to get a negative review removed from Amazon. Oh, by the way, God, if you are reading this story, I am still waiting for *that* miracle.

One night, I simply lost it and began to tweet back to the guy. No one has ever accused me of being boring and I can promise you that I used my wicked sense of humor to comment on his statements about me. Something quite amazing happened in rather short order. Instead of being depressed and tearful like I was when I began my rampage, I found myself laughing and actually having the best time. I was reminded of the teachings of Ester and Jerry Hicks where they said that your feelings were your emotional guidance system and you should always "follow your joy." I was joyful in that moment. Right or wrong, it became clear to me that my inner child really wanted to beat up this bully.

I was done being the victim.

I discovered I was a quick learner and was actually better at being a troll than my nemesis. I created several parody Twitter accounts that tweeted his words back to him with a sarcastic commentary. He had given me a lot of material to work with because most of the things he tweeted bordered upon deranged. People eventually noticed and began laughing with me. I "borrowed" his picture, like he had done mine, but instead of calling him old, fat, and ugly like he called me, I used it to create some quite amusing pictures. I reciprocated his cybersquatting and trying to direct people away from my website, and with the help of a friend, I purchased his dot coms. He had obtained the cheaper dot nets, but the dot coms were available. I do not think he appreciated the creativity I invested in his new dot com websites. Suddenly, after seeing them, he was willing to negotiate and stop all of this nonsense.

He got beat up by a girl, pure and simple.

Sometimes to stop a bully, you have to speak their language to stop them. They want you to be weak and do not know what to do when you stand up to them. Sometimes a good ass-kicking is exactly what they need.

Time has a way of giving you the ability to look at something in a different light. What I have learned from this experience is that being spiritual does not mean I always have to turn the other cheek. Sometimes I have to stand up to evil people and allow my inner warrior to fight. I realized I was not only fighting for myself, but also for the people down the road he might attempt to bully in the future. Hopefully, his experience with me will make him think twice.

This experience also taught me the power of our words and how they can inflict pain. It has made me even more aware of the power of what I say. It has taught me to pay attention to what I see on social media, and, if I see someone being bullied, I do not pass by without giving a word of encouragement. It has also helped to heal my inner child who felt so helpless in the past, and it has empowered me to reject the victim mentality I was programmed with. I now consider myself an anti-bully advocate.

In the end, I thank my troll friend for the experience because it helped me to grow mentally, emotionally, and spiritually.

I also want you to know that God and I are just fine.

SHE LEARNS THE BEAUTY IN PAIN

By Brenda Quintero-Lombardi

The beauty in pain is real. Pain is a very real, raw emotion that takes time to fully understand. It is the soul's way of telling us that we need to start over, change and re-ignite our hearts. Because of my pain, I have more beauty and wholeness in my life now than I ever imagined being able to possess. I credit it to my experiences and my surrender to my Higher Power, which to me is God.

My pain began at the age of 12. A family member suffered from severe mental illness which was later diagnosed as bi-polar disorder. I grew up feeling fear that stemmed from their drastic mood swings that went from the highs of a euphoric "I love the world!" to the lows of "I am going to scream, yell, and break everything in sight!" I remember that during the worst of it, my parents were even afraid. Imagine being a child and the two people whom you look to for protection can't even control the situation.

The worst night was when I saw my father get

pushed down half a flight of stairs. I watched, hopeless and petrified. From that day on, my childhood was gone. To endure this household I was taught to be a good girl and be quiet. Stay in your room, do not be the cause of the mood swings, and do not express your emotions. My world was silent on the inside and exhausting on the outside.

Finally, at the age of 20, I was able to go off to college and get an education. I felt free.

But freedom was very scary at first. I no longer had to hold back anything. I did not have to pretend to smile. I did not have to be quiet. It took me a while to get used to feeling that it was okay to express myself. So I cracked open in a very bad way. I began to go out and drink heavily. I had no true identity or self-esteem so my self-worth was extremely low. Only by the grace of God did I not end up addicted to drugs, unexpectedly pregnant, or worse. After college I became what I like to call a functional "low-steemer." Instead of self-esteem, I had "low-steem." Yep, I coined that phrase just for you.

I got my first job after graduating and was able to keep my incredible low-steem hidden. In fact, some people might be surprised reading this to know that. After a long-term relationship ended in 2012, I cracked even more. I moved to a big city, took a job, and isolated myself for two years. I did not want to face this cruel, bitch of a world that had betrayed me and let me become this pathetic person. I was sad, alone, and I had settled for being content with this life. Settling for being content with a life that isn't truly yours is the worst thing you can do to yourself.

In 2014, I came clean to my family. I let them know I was unhappy, depressed, and needed a change. They had all moved to Florida while I had remained in Texas.

They told me I should move to Florida, too, and I did. I thought it would be a positive life change. In Florida, I found a great opportunity and began a new life chapter. I was letting myself start over, be unknown, and be able to write a new story. I should have felt empowered, important, and needed as I helped more than thirty people manage their businesses. I was surrounded by their positive words, lust for life, and an entrepreneurial spirit for the real estate business.

People kept telling me I was destined for great things, yada yada, and since I couldn't believe them, I began to isolate myself and cracked open even more. This time I developed an anxiety disorder. My anxiety came from trying to live up to everyone's expectations of me. I felt I had to be perfect for everyone. At the age of 32, I moved back in with my parents and took several months off to reflect: How did I get here? Why am I failing? Why isn't Florida different for me?

I sought out a therapist in Cocoa Beach and she helped me gain perspective. I saw that I had spent so much of my life monitoring my actions and words that I had never really been able to have a set identity or express myself in healthy ways. She told me it was a common condition, and that women more often than men feel the pressure to be perfect and adhere to others expectations. After months of therapy, I realized one important lesson: I, and only I, am the creator of my destiny. I, and only I, can CHOOSE to be happy, whole and believe I am worth love. I gave myself permission to stop pretending and start living.

So I did.

I focused on what I wanted out of my life, and started crying and praying. That might sound crazy but try it! If you feel pain at this very moment, close your eyes, find your dark place, allow it to surface, and cry it out of your body. Now open your eyes, raise your arms to the sky, and cry your way to happiness and freedom through tears of gratitude, joy, and surrender. Truly surrender yourself to your Higher Power and let Him be your guide. I surrender my pain daily to find the beauty of my soul's yearning. I am not perfect and still struggle daily, but when I have moments of weakness, I say words of gratitude out loud. I find my happy place and I continue on my journey.

I am now happily married to a wonderful man who shows me incredible love. I run two businesses of my own. I am proud to own my heart and have the courage to grow. Pain is a very real emotion that is created out of fear. Do not fear your destiny; the beauty in your soul will call to you. LET IT IN!

SHE FOLLOWS HER STARS
TO DEEPER ENLIGHTENMENT

By Dominique Jaramillo

I call my first conscious experience of my true Self my "Popeye Moment." This breakthrough occurred during an enlightenment intensive where I spent three days asking the question, "Who Am I?" After two days of alternating every 10 minutes between contemplation and asking the question of myself, and then sitting witness for another person's inquiry, I finally said, "I don't know! I am what I am!"

Yes! It was that simple! I felt this surge come up from my gut, and before I knew it, I was bent over in bliss, holding my stomach, laughing hysterically. I remember walking around the retreat center that night vibrating from head to toe. I laid on the grass looking up at the stars feeling totally connected to everything above and below me, and yet completely free and liberated. I was on a natural high and I never wanted to come down. I finally had a visceral experience of God, Universal Love, and my Self as That! *I am what I am.*

But enlightenment is as fleeting as it is spontaneous. You can have a profound epiphany about who you are in a moment and be forever changed. But in order for a new truth to be fully realized, and the benefits of it sustained in any real way in daily life, one must keep asking and moving through the layers of pain and struggle that come up to challenge that truth.

When I was a young girl, I had two posters in my room. One said "Love to Be Loved" with hearts, and the other said "Aquarius", my Sun sign, with a long list of characteristics of that zodiac sign. I liked a lot of those qualities: friendly, fun, independent, original. And some didn't resonate with me at all. I wondered if one day I might become those other things, or if maybe it was all wrong and astrology was just the silly taboo most people thought it was. Or was I missing something, because why wasn't the other poster in my room that touched me so deeply on the list of descriptions?

From an early age, I was already seeking and asking the big questions: Who am I? What am I? Why am I here? What is God? What is Love? Until now, I had looked in all kinds of places outside of myself for the answers. I watched movies; explored traditional religions; studied the Kabbalah; and read endless books like *Conversations with God, Many Lives, Many Masters, The Seat of The Soul,* along with many other self-help books, including *Men are from Mars, Women are from Venus.* I tested my worth through relationships and confronted my fears through adventures like skydiving. And seven years before this life-altering experience of asking *Who am I?* I had moved across the country to Los Angeles in the hopes of fulfilling my childhood dream of becoming an actress.

However, after struggling for about five years with

very few successful moments, being heartbroken by a man I thought I might marry, and spending most of my time working at a local restaurant, I began feeling like a complete failure. I needed something to change, and fast. So I quit dating, quit acting, and quit waitressing. I got a typical 9-to-5 job, and for the first time in my life, I had a consistent income and a sense of security. I was learning new things I was good at and I also had lots of free time on my hands. So when a friend suggested that I should take a class in something that interested me, the first thing that came to mind was astrology.

As I began my studies, I immediately felt enlightened and validated by finally having the complete picture of my natal birth chart. I learned quickly that astrology goes way beyond the Sun sign and that we are each a unique energy combination of the entire zodiac. The Sun sign may hold the key to the Soul's destiny and who we are becoming in this life, but the rest of the birth chart can indicate the type of terrain that we will be called upon to travel to get there. Everyone goes through the same planetary cycles throughout life, but we each experience them in different ways, positively or negatively, based on our unique personalities, level of self-awareness, and our personal choices.

It became very clear to me why I had approached life the way I did; why I was way more emotional than your average Aquarius Sun; and why love, family, learning, and constantly evolving were so important to me. This new knowledge of my universal blueprint refreshed, rejuvenated, and transformed me because, as much as I loved acting, I no longer felt that it was my true purpose or path. I also felt quite empowered to know that my astrology chart did not dictate who I was or would be, but rather, it was a priceless map that could assist me on the journey toward discovering, co-creating, and reaching my ultimate potential.

Astrology further proved it could be a trusted guide when I looked back at my life choices from the perspective of how the planetary energies were in play with my birth chart at each moment. It verified the timing of why I made the huge move across the country to take a crack at my dream when I did; why I wasn't successful; and what pushed me to change directions when energies pointed to the opportunity for expansion through travel, higher learning, and spiritual growth. I jumped at the chance to take two trips to Europe in less than a year, started studying astrology and joined a metaphysical group that used the enlightenment intensives to invoke personal breakthroughs in short amounts of time.

This awakening work culminated in my fourth enlightenment intensive in 18 months. On day four out of five, while asking the question, "What is Love?" I had another breakthrough experience of myself that also came from the gut. I again found myself doubled over in my chair, holding my stomach. But this time a sharp pain began building deep in my lower abdomen. "What is this?" I asked out loud. The pain increased and increased until I felt like I was being possessed by something. Without hesitation I started yelling, "Get it out—get it out of me!"

I was overwhelmed with pain and sadness all at once, and was pushing hard on my stomach. When the pain finally released, I just hung there for a while, holding and rocking myself like an innocent child, crying and saying, "Shhh, it's ok. You're ok. It will all be ok." I slowly gathered myself, wiped away the tears, and sat up in my chair.

I looked across at my intensive partner, who also was my best friend, and asked softly, "What the hell was that? I feel like I just gave birth!" Her face was warm but neutral as she calmly said, "Thank you." When in the role of witness for another in an intensive, you are not to comment, judge, or give advice; a witness simply responds by showing appreciation for the sharing.

I guess I'd been working so hard at trying to "know thy Self" that it appeared to bring me back, in this moment, to the experience of my own birth. I was physically feeling my mom giving birth to me.

As the days and weeks passed, I contemplated the meaning of that self-birth experience by studying the astrology charts of my parents for deeper understanding. I knew their history, but I had never really stopped to think about the circumstances under which I came into the world and the mark that it could have left on me. My father had essentially already left my mother for another woman before I was born. My mother was alone, hurting, heartbroken, and angry. It was a cold, snowy February afternoon and I can only imagine the emotions reeling through her as the pain of childbirth began. She wanted me out so badly because she needed me, as I needed her, to experience true unconditional love. She already had my three-year-old brother, but that had been different because when he was born, she and my dad were different.

Astrology once again came to my aid to help me understand why I would never be able to have the kind of relationship I wanted with my father. I laughed and cried at the same time with this new awareness. Emotionally, I had hung onto my mother's pain as my own pain all my life. I had deeply and unconsciously feared ever giving marriage or motherhood a chance.

Now I understood why.

My mother is a Cancer Sun, the sign that rules the Moon and Motherhood. She was a proud mother and survivor who chose to leave a man and go it alone with two small kids in a time and culture where that wasn't done. She put us, her family, first, regardless of how hard the journey might have been. She was the epitome of sacrifice in the name of Love. Looking back, my mother was always there for me, in good times and especially in bad: supporting me, loving me, and encouraging me to always keep going and to follow my heart.

This rebirth experience gave me the ultimate opportunity to know and be my true Self. I could now separate myself from my parents, their story, and where I came from, and take real steps to build more honest, loving relationships with them both. I now knew my personal value and that I am the only one who determines my worth. I also knew I could do the same thing my mother did if I was faced with similar hardships because you do what you have to do in those situations to save your soul. I felt fortunate to save my soul through seeking and reliving the moment when she saved hers. My mother has been my greatest teacher, guide, and friend, and we continue to support each other every day.

From that moment of revelation, my life was set on a new course. My heart was open and I was free to write my own story.

I began seriously studying astrology and gained more confidence and belief through experience of its service to daily living. Astrology instilled a new kind of love and compassion for myself and others, and showed me what a powerful teacher and tool it can be. I was inspired to become an Astrologer so I could potentially give the same gift of self-knowledge and personal power to others that astrology gave to me.

My life was transformed again when I married the man whom I had met on my first day of that 9-to-5 job years ago. He and I had spoken to each other every day for three years. The timing of our connection felt destined because the Universe kept him in the shadows just long enough for me to really complete the enlightenment journey I was on in order to prepare me for our relationship. Once the divine timing was right, we wasted no time in moving forward. We got married, bought a home, and had a child. Having our son and becoming a mother myself was another experience of pure love that changed me forever. My son is a powerful Pisces Soul, the sign that rules spirituality and unconditional love, and he continues to bless us every day.

Being a wife and mother has been more amazing and enlightening than I could have ever imagined. It is the biggest part of who I am in this life, and it makes me a better person in all areas of my life. I feel very blessed and proud that I found myself, found a true partner, and was able to create this beautiful life I am living. I also feel very grateful that I discovered astrology and have it to support me along the way.

The cycle of life never stops, and the process of growth, self-actualization, and personal discovery never ends—thank goodness! I just have to remember to always trust my gut.

I am a wife, a mother, a daughter, a sister, a friend, an Astrologer.

I am all of these things, and no-thing at all.

I am a Soul in a body having a human experience.

I am Love.
I am God.
I am That.
I am what I am!

SHE FACES HER FEELINGS OF FAILURE

By Devon Telberg

There really isn't any particular event that could be called a tragedy in my life, yet I'm able to talk about failure because enough events have happened that have caused me months and years of thinking about it. At 12 years old, my childhood friend publicly rejected me, and I spent the next year and a half eating lunch in a bathroom stall to avoid the cafeteria. At 16 years old, my first boyfriend dumped me for no reason and triggered another year and a half of feeling alone and lonely. There have been many other stories in my life with the feelings of failure: losing a job, being really poor, losing another relationship. Every few years something happened in my life to trigger a feeling of deep hopelessness and loneliness. Most recently, it was losing two jobs and not being able to find anyone who believed in my abilities.

Writing about the failures in my life makes me feel that they should be over, and that I should have grown past them. But I haven't. The reason I spend so much time in a perceptible depression is actually me holding on to the experiences to analyze them, and make sure they never happen again. I want to be beyond that failed relationship, that failed job, and that failed situation. I have had to take a lot of breaks from being employed just to deal with my emotions; even I can see it's not very constructive. Perhaps I'm too thoughtful for my own good. I'm smart, capable, sufficient, and strong; but I have felt completely debilitated when overly focused on my disappointments. It has gotten to the point where it's overwhelming me. Taking the time for evaluation has been worth it, but only so I can begin to be constructive with my life again.

When I see someone else in a state of perceived failure, it seems that nothing is working for them. It looks like they're just doing the same thing over and over again, hoping for a different result. It looks like they are actually refusing to be successful in order to struggle with something so seemingly simple. I want to tell them how they could try to do things a little differently because I think they just don't know that another way could help them make some progress. I want to say they're doing it wrong because look at the lack of results. I might try to help them to accept whatever it is and move on. An external conversation with another would be like speaking to myself.

But failure feels very different from the inside. It feels like total frustration with everything as I compare my current situation to the image of what I want it to be. It feels like success could be possible if only *one thing* would click into place. It feels lonely when nothing new happens. It feels like doubt when I don't trust the progress that does happen. It feels like emptiness from lack of the *one thing* that I believe would make my life happy.

To me, failure feels like an unrelenting truth that I have convinced myself of. A truth that comes back again and again after I've wondered for too long what else it is that I'm supposed to be doing about it. Listening to this truth means detaching from people who want me to compromise on something in my life that I am fighting for. I have convinced myself that failure will always exist for me, even in a quiet place in the center of my heart.

When I feel debilitated by disappointment, I have discovered that I have the power to decide how long it will last. Closing my eyes, I pray that as long as I confront that day to the best of my ability, something could change. My commitment to being myself and surrendering to the world is actually a form of faith in myself in disguise. I plead with the Universe to please step in; I have done all I could do. I resolve to face the situation faithfully, in my energy. Following my life with conviction can guide me towards everything that I value more deeply.

With this faith and conviction comes simplicity. Flakes of things that do not really matter drop away. It may seem like my life path has narrowed with every choice I made, but the whole picture is that my life's opportunities have expanded. The whole picture, beyond myself, includes progress in the smallest shift of energy. It includes the perspective from the inside and the outside, the dynamic that works together in order to push me toward the purest form of love: love for the insider, myself, and love for the outsider, as I see others.

Letting go of the image of what the path *should* look like has been important as I started to experience what success feels like. At this moment, I am still striving for my idea of happiness. Sometimes when something happens that is not what I want, I actually have to remind myself that I may be restricting the possibility of an opportunity. I've become more aware that I am the one who puts this limit in place, and this awareness opens me up to consider doing it another way instead. Sometimes, I have to go along with what doesn't look like what I want in order to let it progress anyway, still carrying my heart's desire through it. I go along with other possibilities because I am curious to see how it will pan out.

This is how I let other people influence my life. If I really do not wish to limit how my life will be, then I must be open to the possibility of alternative suggestions, incorporating them into my life, and knowing that my identity does not depend on doing everything only one way. I want to be sure to be present in myself because that is what enables me to live my life my way.

Before, I would become debilitated trying to figure out what went wrong while pursuing a goal. Now I know I can hold those questions in my heart, and in some mysterious way, my questions get answered: from a conversation with someone I encounter during my day, or a moment when I just feel relieved of the question's burden. I am no longer afraid or too overwhelmed to prepare for the day. I don't need to stay in bed for an hour before getting up. I can acknowledge the feelings in my heart, and carry them with me as I work through the day. It's not necessary to disclose all the inner arguments; just face that day the way it is, with a deep knowing that what I want is still coming to me.

Taking any step to make a dream real can be terrifying to me because I do not know for certain if it's the right step to take. Looking forward without a path is like a fog that sits at the tip of your nose. When I focus on both sides of my inner debate, moving forward can feel impossible. Then I return to my intention, knowing the right step to take means feeling YES in every drop of my body. I now allow myself to settle into the energy, and sit with it for weeks or months to understand how to move forward. Staying conscious of the opportunities helps me flow with the Universe, while reminding me that I am not alone. Doing and not-doing are both important for the right path. I stop just to think about it, to determine that this small step is sure and grounded in my heart's true desire to create my new life.

Realizing this new level of faith has freed me. I have stopped looking for the next job, the next relationship, the next "right" step. I now have some space to create my life with a calmer, grounding energy. Each job and relationship are just another chapter in my life that lead me forward. Between the chapters, there is empty space to re-adjust and re-focus on the next undertaking. If I have to face the next chapter alone, I just relax. I rest in my convictions; they will guide me. One job does not epitomize my career. One relationship does not define my life. Success is not a final destination. Accepting that everything will be okay once and for all, means accepting that everything is okay right now. Life goes on, energy changes, and the next challenge will pop up.

I fear at times that the same situations will be presented to me over and over again, but this perspective helps me strive to be better. Facing the feeling of failure means being grateful even when I'm not satisfied. The world is infinite and I can decide to change my experience of it at any moment. I'm grateful my feelings are in tune with that. I'm happy to move forward and foster my life from a more grounded place.

On the outside, my life may look uncertain at times, but I'm happy with the strength of my faith and that I am creating a better life to ground my true happiness *for real*. It may take a long time, but that is okay. What else would I strive for in this life? The inner path through failure to my true life is my journey, and my faith is all the stronger for the struggle.

SHE OPENS TO THE POWER
OF HER FEMININITY

By Alice Brooking

So here I sit, a 24 year old pregnant woman who is finally embracing what it means to step into herself and the sacred feminine energy. The continuous journey of self-discovery has led me down many interesting pathways, though they all lead to the same destination... love.

When I was growing up, I had some serious issues with becoming a woman. I couldn't stand it when my mother said "bra" or "bikini." In short, anything that represented womanhood would bring up feelings of shame. I would stare at myself in the mirror and feel a deep-seated guilt for being in a woman's body.

In my teen years I had no respect for myself. I just didn't care. I was ungrounded, drinking too much, doing too many substances, and eating terrible food, all with the mindset of "woe is me." I was working as a bartender surrounded by people practicing the same unhealthy habits. I met my ex-partner when I was 18. He didn't drink, smoke, or do drugs and that pulled me right out of the dark hole I had dug for myself. The two of us moved back to our small home town and away from the city. This is when the magic started to happen for me.

I began to hear the whispers of my heart again. It took me a little while to listen to the gentle voice of my intuition but I finally heard it. I cut down on the partying, read spiritually-based books, and became mindful of my thoughts and how they created my reality. The conscious journey began. Things that used to resonate with me simply didn't anymore. People, environments, food, and drinks I used to love no longer did it for me. I realized I had been in denial about who I was. That denial came from the shame I felt for being a woman, and my struggle with self-acceptance.

It was time to start respecting myself. How can anyone respect me if I can't even respect myself? I have always been very kind-hearted and caring towards others, but my own self-talk was the exact opposite. Self-love became my focus and by doing this, my care and love for others naturally became more pronounced.

Meat and dairy were no longer resonating with my body so I stopped eating them. Substance abuse became less and less desirable. My self-talk was becoming more positive and encouraging. Speaking, doing, and living MY truth became my way of being and it still is.

Astrology and numerology helped me to understand myself even more. I gained an understanding of the human psyche which was incredibly helpful. Insight became my new drug of choice. The more love I allowed in, the more my world opened up.

I had always been one to apologize for everything. I realized I had been apologizing for being me, not wanting to inconvenience anyone by my mere presence. To allow myself to be unapologetically *me* was empowering on so many levels.

Letting go has been a tough one, especially being a Cancer sun sign in astrology. My past relationship had tested that to the extreme, pushing me to my limits, breaking through the barriers and back into the flow of life. I gained acceptance that everything, right in this very moment, is perfect and going exactly to divine plan.

I am perfect in this very moment and everything that has happened in my life has brought me to now. I love myself now so I love everything that has come before.

Every aspect of our lives has a higher purpose. Sometimes, when we are experiencing something we perceive to be "not in our favor," it actually IS in our favor. Everything happens for our highest good; to learn and grow as a soul in a physical body.

With this realization, I got to a point where I looked around at all this personal work I had done and I recognized I had inadvertently changed myself to a degree that I was not living in alignment with my inner truth. My partner at the time was searching for something and wanted to test an open relationship. This had been years in the making and I had finally convinced myself that it could work. I changed my morals in the process of accommodating his preferences. My partner and I both recognized that we were at a stalemate, and this brought up yet another fundamental question for me. My heart and intuition were saying "Trust that you are divinely guided." My head was saying "You're crazy?!"

My heart won and I followed my intuition. I just HAD to. I was yearning for new experiences and was ready to embrace change.

Breaking up with someone you deeply care for takes courage, and I do applaud myself for that. It was the end of a cycle and we both recognized it on many levels. Even though it was difficult, there was an underlying ease as my heart was leading the way. I was flowing in the ever-changing nature of existence.

During this process I had come across the absolute opposite side of myself, my "twin flame" as some call it. Yin and yang, the ultimate feminine and masculine relationship in terms of two spirits coming together in sacred union. My twin flame is the ultimate masculine which allows me to embrace the ultimate feminine within myself. The love and connection we have is humbling and I honor it.

I now feel there is such beauty and strength in being a woman. I had denied myself this realization for too long. Feminine energy is all over my numerology and astrology charts and I'm finally stepping into it. My intuition has heightened. I feel at peace with myself and my nurturing qualities. I'm even dressing in a more feminine way.

So here I sit, carrying the embodiment of our twin flame love in my womb, amazingly creating life, and BEing love. I sit in gratefulness for every aspect of my life. I am being provided the experiences that are just right for me in this moment. I trust this moment is perfect as the divine knows what it's doing.

We are all the divine. Trust in that and all will be well, no matter what happens.

SHE SURRENDERS TO
NOT KNOWING THE PATH AHEAD

By Erika Elmuts

My husband woke up, turned over in bed, and announced our marriage was over.

In a matter of days, I had packed up my entire life, moved myself and my daughter into a new home, regrouped, and began anew. I had gone from having a roof over my head, a partner who supported my vision, and being able to focus on being a mom and building my business, to having less than five months of living expenses in the bank from my marriage settlement.

At the time of that unexpected divorce, I had thankfully discovered my life's purpose and passion: helping families live healthier and more abundant lives. I was a regularly featured expert on local news stations in San Diego. I had been on a national television talk show and numerous radio shows, and was collaborating with other thought leaders in my industry. The seeds I had planted in the early years had begun to sprout, and it was an exciting time.

After my divorce, I continued to follow my business plan, which was to continue to build my online community of parents and launch my parenting course that I had been working on for almost a year. I had more television and radio appearances. I was interviewed on NBC's *The Today Show*, and *The New York Times* asked me to write an article. I saw all of those opportunities as a sign that I was in alignment with what I was here to contribute to the world, and my task was to show up, work, and trust what came my way.

Meanwhile, money was always on my mind. I had a deadline to monetize my work by finally launching my course that I had developed with my heart and soul, and really needed to establish a regular income. By 2014, I had lined up four massive opportunities. If any one of these four came to fruition, I would be in great financial shape. Except that didn't happen.

A check for $3,500 that was coming my way, suddenly didn't and threw me into an immediate tailspin. My energy shifted instantaneously since that check was the difference between continuing on this path and launching my product, or not having enough money to pay my bills.

I went from being hopeful, empowered, excited, and eager, to not sleeping a wink at night, judging myself harshly for being in this situation, questioning my path, and feeling desperate. In that energetic shift into panic and desperation, it's not surprising that all of those four opportunities I had lined up fell through at the eleventh hour. I felt like I was 95 yards down the field, so close to reaching my goal. The safety of the end zone was within view. Except for months, I remained frozen at the 95 yard line with those four major possibilities that would have secured me financially and professionally, staying out of reach.

From the outside, I looked like I had it all. I was a success in many people's eyes, someone who people listened to and who people wanted to hear from. The on-going inquiries I had from the media and other enterprises were indicators that I had something going, that I had something to offer, and people were drawn to my messages.

But what people didn't know was how close I was to losing my home. Just when I thought things were at their bleakest and I had exhausted all of my solutions, I received an unexpected $100 from a friend who knew I was struggling financially. Then I got a call from another friend wanting to hire me for a few hours to do some work for her, which just so happened to pay the exact amount I needed to make to avoid losing my home.

I had even tried crowdfunding to raise money for my business and got some pledges towards my goal. But I fell short, which meant losing all of the pledged money. I was devastated. A few days later, one of my friends, who had pledged to support me at the $500 level, sent me the check anyway because she believed in what I was doing.

Finally, I simply surrendered to not knowing. I practiced being open when I felt so much fear that I was constricted spiritually and physically all the time. My surrender to the process, and really trying to be comfortable with not being in control, is what I know helped me survive.

I then gave up my life's passion, which I had worked so hard to build, so that I could "do the right thing": I accepted a full-time job and temporarily traded in my dreams for stability and responsibility.

After I started the job, I began to see the toll it was taking on my daughter since I was expected to work nights and weekends. Soon I was working until 11 p.m. on some weeknights, and many Saturday mornings as well. I had no time for self-care or time to be with my daughter, to help her with her homework, or to make dinner together like we always had.

I had gone from having sovereignty over my time and schedule, to having no flexibility and having my personal family time taken from me. While having this job was the "right thing to do" financially, it came at a substantial cost: my daughter's well-being, as well as my own.

For most of her life, my seven-year-old daughter had a mom who was present. Because I had been self-employed, I was able to fit my work in when she was at school, or after she went to bed. One of my core values is presence, which means that when I am with her, I am *with her*. I am not on the phone, not multi-tasking, and not shoving a device in front of her so I can get things done.

The moment I took that job, things changed.

Now when I picked her up at school, I was hurried. When I dropped her off, I was in a rush. I was stressed out having to leave work briefly to pick her up. Once we got home, I was back on the computer, being Skyped while I was on a Zoom video meeting, and my phone was blowing up with text messages at the same time. The pace of my life was at full tilt—and my daughter was witness to her mom changing in front of her eyes. I became more impatient, less tolerant, I didn't laugh much anymore, and I had nothing to give since I was maxed out. My face reflected the tension I was living day to day.

The more stressed out I became, the more she needed my attention and connection, and I had very little to give her. The stress I was under with this job took more of a toll on me than the stress of financial hardship and single motherhood. I had traded one massive stressor for an even worse one.

Even though I could now pay the bills, the "right thing" didn't feel so right anymore.

I felt like I was on a high-speed train with no option to get off or to stop and think. I was in reactive mode constantly and no longer in control of my life. And I hated the feeling that I had zero bandwidth to work on my passion business that I had been building for years, so that literally came to an abrupt halt.

I felt completely trapped.

The two things that fed my soul — being a present mother and living my life's purpose in my work — were gone from my life. I felt hollow, empty, and stressed. The light had left me. I felt like a black and white version of myself, rather than the Technicolor version that I had been before and needed to be again.

As the job progressed, I had spent the previous two weeks, including weekends, in preparation for a massive event. Even though all my ideas had been shot down as "too innovative," I worked 15–17 hour days to finish up this huge project. Not surprisingly to me, the event did not live up to expected revenue projections. Around 9 p.m. that evening, in the midst of a perceived failure, an unexpected sense of peace came over me. I set my intention that within six months, I would be free from this job. I knew, beyond a shadow of a doubt, that I would find a way to own my time again. I didn't know how I would do it, or what it would look like; I just knew that within six months, I would find a way to leave the job and take back my life. I set that intention with the ferocity of a mama bear, and the belief that I would accomplish it. There was nothing—I mean NOTHING—that would stop me from finding a way.

What was different about this time was that my intention came from a visceral place—a place deep down inside of me that declared, "That's enough!" It was not an option. There was no middle ground of "Maybe I can set some boundaries, just do the best I can, and that's all I can do."

There was zero doubt in my mind. I wanted, and needed, to have a better life.

Flash forward only three months. I had manifested an opportunity that aligned with my values and offered me a larger platform upon which to spread my message to thousands of healthy families across the world, not to mention a life that fit me in a much more balanced way.

The exhilaration I experienced when I gave my notice to leave the job is like nothing I had ever experienced before. For me that step represented far more spiritually than could be observed from the outside. I had an undeniable sense of empowerment, knowing that I had found a way to not sacrifice the well-being of my family for money, or for doing the "right" and responsible thing. I know there is a way I can do the right thing AND maintain my values of presence and connection with my family.

And I made it happen.

Reflecting back on that time now, I recognize my breakthrough moment was when I claimed my power to live from a place of connection and abundance, and not let fear dictate my choices. I had no idea how I would make it happen when I made that declaration, but I knew I would. There was no angst, no doubt, no cerebral strategizing or planning. It was complete surrender to allowing the right things to come my way, and having the courage to surrender to it.

The old me would need to know the steps, the "how," the A to B to C that would get me to the goal. This time, it was different. I had no clue, yet I was living from my inner knowing and silencing my mind. I felt calm, and at peace—while being fiercely determined. I just knew from the depths of my soul that I would get there.

And I did.

As strange as it seems, it is not always up to us to figure out the "how" of a situation. There are times when the Universe will take care of that missing piece as long as we set a clear intention for what we ultimately desire.

Then—and this is the hardest part of all—we have to let go of the need to control the outcome. Instead, surrender, allow, and trust. Know your core values and what you cannot compromise on in your life. Take inspired action, and things will unfold in the most magical of ways when you stay open to the many paths to get there.

SHE CHOOSES HER NEXT LIFE VISION

By Lauren Goldstein

*W*hat do I want? Those four little words were something that I never really gave any great thought to until about eight months ago. I finally realized that I had spent the past 29 years of my life on auto-pilot without really noticing it. Then someone asked me what I wanted, and I was lost. I had no idea where to start. I guess sometimes in order to start, you have to go back, so let me take you back in time to where my first life dream began.

I was four years old and sitting on the plush carpet of my bedroom with my childhood dog, Murphy, sitting patiently in front of me. A stethoscope was in my ears as I listened intently to his heart, with a line of stuffed animal patients waiting for Dr. Lauren to check them next. I was practicing being a doctor on this captive audience since it was what I wanted to be when I grew up. Well, I *thought* I wanted to be a doctor; I really just wanted to help people. So at the ripe age of four, I thought it was my only option in life and it stuck. It stuck until I was 24.

I had dedicated all of my academic life, volunteer hours, and even my heart to the medical field. Yes, I had pigeonholed myself, but I had it all planned out. I was going to be a pediatrician, marry a wonderful man, raise babies and Labradors together, and drive matching Land Rovers. This was going to be a breeze.

Fast forward to a typical Tuesday when I was now working at Children's Hospital Colorado. The smell of warm pancakes wafted through the lobby, children played in the waiting areas, and the elevator hummed as I made my way up to the Epileptic Monitoring Unit (EMU). Today was my clinical day, a welcome retreat from the research lab. I was on my way to the EMU to accompany my boss, the Chief of Neurology, and our medical residents on rounds. I was lucky enough to be in the only Level 1 trauma children's hospital in the Rocky Mountain Region, so I saw some truly amazing things. I was granted permission to be in the operating room during an awake craniotomy, witnessed the rare anomaly of mirror twins, and rejoiced in seeing kids recover from dire health situations. I was in love with medicine, with the kiddos at the hospital, and with the dream I had planted twenty years earlier. But all of that was about to change on this February morning.

I had just received my latest rejection letter from medical school the day before, but I still had some lingering hope. On that Tuesday morning, we had a baby come in in a very critical epileptic state. We saved her and put her on a 10-day treatment plan to get her to a full recovery that would give this precious little five month old girl her best chance of a normal life without seizures. But by 11 a.m., it officially became the day I lost faith in everything I had planned for in my life. The insurance company said *no* to her treatment.

After all of our best work and advice, we were told that they had decided not to cover the 10-day treatment, and we would need to take her off the medication immediately. I saw a baby caught in the crossfire, as her mother felt helpless for her infant's life, and all of us feeling equally helpless as an insurance company made a horrible cost/benefit analysis decision. This child could have had a good life, but because the insurance company said no, the little girl's future now weighed in the balance with huge medical costs and ongoing severe seizures being the most likely scenario for her life. I wish I could say that we ultimately convinced the insurance company to change their mind and this story had a happy ending, but it did not. That moment of *not* being able to help someone in need is frozen in time for me as the moment that my life direction fell apart. I couldn't spend the next six years of my life training to be in a field where I was unable to do what was best for my patients because an insurance company had the power to say *no*. I felt paralyzed. I remember sadness sweeping over me, then anger from wasted time crushing my very soul, and saying to myself F*CK! Now what?

Interestingly, it wasn't so much that I didn't get into medical school that upset me about this direction change; statistically, it is HARD to get into medical school. And it wasn't necessarily that one tiny baby's future was now uncertain. What really came up was that I now felt like an utter failure. I had wrapped my whole self-worth around this one dream. When I realized this was no longer where my life was going, I felt like a failure because I didn't know what else to pursue next. In my mind, failure was the real-life embodiment of being lost and uncertain. I had spent so long focused on this dream and embodying this path, that when I looked in the mirror, I realized I had no idea who I was anymore.

I had always clung to the saying that "Everything happens for a reason," but I did not see a reason yet. I had no idea what direction to go next since medicine was clearly not my calling. In order to stay busy, I ramped up my Rodan and Fields skincare business, became a part-time nanny, and got a part-time job at Nordstrom as a personal stylist (mostly for the discount because who doesn't love Nordstrom.)

Then I wallowed and cried because I was still lost. I felt like I had no identity; like I was nothing. I wanted to help people, I wanted to make a difference, and I had walked away from the only occupation I had ever wanted or known. What was I thinking? Did I make a giant mistake? Would I ever be as happy as when I walked through those hospital doors every day, looking at the children we helped make better (insurance companies be damned)? Would I ever find my true calling?

The demons I wrestled with for months were self-doubt, pity, grief, victimhood, and self-loathing. There was no room for self-love in my life. I felt like I had nothing to be proud of. I wasn't who I thought I was. I was an empty shell of a person, wandering through life with expressionless eyes.

I thought that moving to another place would shake me out of my trance and awaken something—anything—in me. When my lease ended in Colorado, I moved to Dallas, thinking my demons surely wouldn't follow me there. I was wrong. It turns out they always follow you, and when you don't have the comfort of the familiar, they get even bigger.

Dallas was the first place I had lived outside of my home state of Colorado. I hoped that a clean slate was just what I needed, and it ultimately was, but it took a long time to emerge from the darkness. Externally, I did my best to put on the mask of "everything is great" but as soon as that front door closed, the darkness crept in again.

Then one night, as I sat on my patio wrapped in a blanket, drinking my favorite tea, and looking at the moon reflecting off the light dusting of snow on the apartments across the street, I finally realized something that would break me out of this trance. I had a choice. I could choose to stay miserable and feel worthless, or I could shift my perspective, pick myself up, and move forward. I chose the latter. I never knew it snowed in Dallas, but *He* knows how much I love snow, so I think it was a sign from God that it was time for another fresh start.

I eventually moved from Dallas to San Francisco, and then back to Texas. I have settled in Austin for the moment, wondering where my next wanderlust impulse might take me. I have read about 50 books on everything having to do with self-improvement, finding your purpose, and spiritual gurus; I have an insatiable appetite for anything and everything about personal and professional development. I was slowly feeling like I was moving away from being a boat without a rudder to someone who was designing her future. I started a consulting business and I built up my amazing Rodan and Fields business even more, but I still missed working with children and being in the medical field. Something was missing. Then that one question changed everything. Again.

"What do you want?"

Five years after leaving the hospital, my mentor asked me this question. Honestly, I didn't have an answer. I immediately thought of what I "should" say, but I couldn't make the words come out. I had absolutely no idea what I wanted. My mentor said, "Don't answer, just think about it tonight, sleep on it, and tell me tomorrow."

I would love to say that I had a brilliant answer when the sun came up the next day, but I didn't. The truth was, I had spent my life in a type of unconscious auto-pilot. I was going down the path I thought I *should* go down to help people. I was doing what my family said I *should* do. I was leaning into what society told me I *should* do. I was drowning in an ocean of "shoulds."

So I asked myself that question every day for two weeks and waited for an answer. In no particular order, this is what I got. I want to:

Have a family
Have financial freedom
Have infinite abundance
Have laughter
Have love
Have joy
Have more friendship
Have more adventure
Travel the world
Break out of the box
Make a difference
Be an inspiring leader
Impact lives for the better
Help people live better lives

There it was on paper — the life that I wanted. It was beautiful to see this list in front of me, only to realize that none of my answers said "Be a doctor" or "Be a consultant" or any other job title. Everything on the list was about *feelings*.

I still had no idea what I wanted to be when I grew up, but I could make another choice. I could choose to only do things in my life that made me feel these feelings and focus on these outcomes. I felt the shackles of the "shoulds" that had enslaved me all my life falling away. I felt myself getting a little braver, a little more open, and feeling a whole lot lighter.

Since this revelation of what I really wanted, I would love to tell you that everything magically fell into place and that it's all been rainbows and sunshine. But it hasn't. I know that my road has been bumpy. There have been many times when I have questioned my existence and have felt so powerless it hurts. There are still days when I have to choose light over darkness, remind myself how powerful I really am, and love myself a little more than usual. As cliché as this saying is, I believe that things fall apart so better things can fall together.

When I look back at the five years since I made the radical life choice to leave the medical field, and the eight months it took to figure out what I wanted, I realize that all along I had the power to choose what I want. I have always had the power — I just let circumstances and other people take it away because I was too scared I would disappoint everyone, including myself. I never fully explored what I truly wanted because I didn't know what I wanted. I also was so unsure of what tomorrow brought that I let fear paralyze me and I got stuck on autopilot.

The woman writing this story for you today is

infinitely different than the woman who walked away from her first love, medicine. I have loved, lost, triumphed, failed, felt lost, and wondered what all of this is about—perhaps you can relate to that rollercoaster? Through the happiness, joy, pain, hurt, and darkness, the truth remains simple: we have the power to choose what we want. At any moment you can decide when enough is enough. You can choose to have a different today than you did yesterday. You can shift your perspective and slaughter your demons.

Today is the day you can choose to live with less fear, more courage; less structure, more flow; less constriction, more opening; less "should do" and more want to; less for their approval, more for your approval; less of have to, more of love to. Remember, only you have your unique gifts, passions and influences. This world needs your light so let it shine on and illuminate your power.

You, and only you, have the power to choose your life and preside over your journey even when your purpose does not feel fully defined.

Oh, and one more secret, lean in close…

…you're not alone…

SHE HEALS

{ Health, Healing, and Wellbeing }

"At this time, when she is releasing and surrendering,
Spirit will dance and sing
and guide her on with angelic presence.
Spirit will show her resources, teachers, and nurturing
moments of peace that affirm the surrender.
She will be given little joys and unexpected
opportunities along the way to coax her forward with
love and reassurance."

The Modern Heroine's Journey of Consciousness

SHE HEALS WITH PURE ACCEPTANCE

By Laren Watson

I sat on the edge of the bulkhead looking out across the Puget Sound. The tide was in so there was no beach on that bright sunny summer day, just water lapping gently against the concrete wall. Across the water, I saw the dense green trees of Maury Island. I took a deep breath and closed my eyes.

My friend had invited me down to her beach-front home to meditate by myself. She was away for the weekend and had offered her backyard as a very soothing place. I readily accepted. I was in need of quiet since only the week before, I had received the shock of my life. I had been diagnosed with stage four mantle cell non-Hodgkins lymphoma, a rare, aggressive, and hard to treat variety of blood cancer. Mantle cell usually affects men over 65. I was 48, female, and a Holistic Health Coach. Not the usual patient profile, that much we knew. I ate entirely organic food, exercised regularly, practiced yoga, meditated, and had a basically happy life with my husband, two kids, and sweet dog. It didn't make sense. I was in shock and reeling from the profound betrayal of my super healthy lifestyle. *How could this have happened to me?*

With the water view surrounding me, I crossed my legs, put my hands in my lap and began to meditate. Focusing on my breath, in and out, I decided to ask a question that I had read in a book as a centering thought, *"What does my body need to heal?"*

I thought this might help me tune in and focus on some possibilities during my planned 30-minute meditation. Getting more rest or switching from coffee to green tea came to mind as things that might help my body to heal from this shocking cancer invasion. What happened during the meditation, though, was something that had never happened to me before. As I asked the question, *"What does my body need to heal?"* I immediately got an answer inside my head. But not the answer I was expecting.

What I heard inside my head on that sunny afternoon was *"Pure Acceptance."*

Pure Acceptance? What is Pure Acceptance? I immediately asked. *"Acceptance of what or of whom? And what does "Pure" mean?"* No further answers came. I got chills as I came to realize this answer didn't come from me. I couldn't have come up with this since I was so confused by it. I sat there in my friend's backyard and quietly freaked out.

I wasn't brought up with any kind of religion and had never been particularly spiritual. I thought religion and spirituality were fine for other people, but I had found enough things that didn't work for me in all of the major religions that I had never wanted to join any of them. I had not ruled out the possibility of a Higher Power, although I did find it hard to believe in one. I was, and continue to be, generally skeptical and proof-driven. Faith was just too much of a leap for me. But here I was hearing an answer that was not my own.

Needless to say, I wasn't really meditating anymore at this point. I was sitting and thinking. Do I follow this advice? Do I start some kind of inquiry into what Pure Acceptance means? How do I apply this to my life? Could there be the possible reward of this somehow healing my body? But whom or what am I supposed to accept?

I decided to just go with it. I would play this out. What did I have to lose? I was facing a serious diagnosis and was willing to give anything a shot. If the Universe / Spirit / God / Source, whatever you call it, was telling me that Pure Acceptance was what my body needed to heal, who was I to argue? But since I hadn't gotten any further instructions, I realized that I would have to work it out myself.

Later that night, I sat down to journal, a practice I had started again with the cancer diagnosis. I chose to start with accepting the people in my life exactly as they are. As I wrote, I found this was not an easy task. Starting close to home, I began writing pages and pages about accepting the people in my family. It turned out to be a laundry list of every character flaw I could think of. I had an inkling this was not how it was supposed to go. This didn't feel like healing. It felt harsh and judgmental. And geez, did I hold people to a high standard! What must it be like to live with me — someone whose standards are so high that you are constantly disappointing them? Ick. Could I turn this acceptance thing back onto myself and accept this lovely character flaw of mine? Not too easily, but I tried.

The next step seemed to be forgiveness. I needed to

forgive all of these people, including myself, for not being perfect, for not living up to my impossible standards, for basically being human. So I wrote about that in my journal. I immediately felt a lightness and a peacefulness in my heart. Maybe I was on to something.

This lesson of Pure Acceptance kept coming up through the following months of treatment as I was forced to give up all control of my life, my schedule, and my agenda. I quite literally turned my life over to my doctors, doing whatever they said to do. I combined the conventional medicine treatments with alternative supplements and recommendations from my naturopathic oncologist. I continued practices that I knew would help, such as eating healing foods, meditation and yoga, staying optimistic, moderate exercise, and gratitude journaling.

But I continued to struggle with Acceptance. I'm a planner. I find comfort in knowing what is going to happen by making a plan and then having things go according to that plan. I am not a control freak, but this serious cancer treatment had thrown me into a whirlwind of appointments every week, all dictated by the doctors' schedules with no regard for how I felt about it. I was on a seriously scary roller coaster and was being told to let go of the handrail and trust that they knew what they were doing.

I was scheduled for four rounds of treatments, each three weeks apart and requiring five-day hospital stays with chemo on continuous drip. After the third round, I was to have my stem cells harvested for a stem cell transplant, a drastic procedure of wiping out my entire immune system and basically replacing it with a new one. They needed to collect five million stem cells and I had already gone through the exhausting procedure once, only getting one and a half million. When the call came the night after the second attempt, the nurse told me that they had only gotten another one and a half million cells, not reaching the five million mark on that try either. The timing of the "harvesting" was a very short window. If we didn't get all that they needed right then, a transplant wouldn't be in my future. She told me that I would need to come in that night for a shot in my belly that would hopefully kick my bone marrow in gear, followed directly by a third attempt.

Well, it was Halloween. I had missed every single one of my daughter's basketball games that Fall due to either being in the hospital or recovering from the chemo. I so wanted to go around the neighborhood with her and her friends and their parents, my friends, and just feel normal. I was bald by then and I had purchased an electric blue wig to wear. I liked the idea of blending in with all of the other wigs and masks. Halloween was one night when people wouldn't necessarily see me as a cancer patient. So I very matter-of-factly told the nurse that "tonight doesn't work for me." There was a pause as my words registered on the other end of the line. She then responded firmly, "You have to come in tonight. We are trying to save your life." And I decided this was another thing I had to yield to. Pure Acceptance once again.

In the end, I accepted the treatment schedule fully. I also had to accept the side effects of the treatment, such as being bald and the fatigue and weakness I felt when I had always been strong and healthy. I had to accept not being the kind of attentive mother I was used to being as I accepted the kindness and generosity of my friends taking over a lot of tasks I used to handle with ease. I also accepted awkward comments and glances from friends and strangers as I lost the hair on my head and weight off my body.

I accepted the fact that some people whom I thought would be there for me really weren't. I let it all go and I accepted people for the imperfectly beautiful people they were.

Was this the Pure Acceptance that the Universe had instructed? I didn't know. Is this what made me able to survive not only this first bout with lymphoma but a second diagnosis right on its heels: stage two triple-negative breast cancer requiring a bilateral mastectomy and more chemo? I didn't know that either. I do know that it helped me find peace during a very difficult period. The alternative would have been resistance and that certainly wouldn't have been helpful.

Accepting all that happened didn't mean that I liked it, condoned it, or approved of it. I just surrendered to the process. I let go and handed my life over to others. I also let go of any negative feelings I had about it, like the fear and the sadness and the occasional insensitive remark. I focused on, and worked hard at, staying optimistic and seeing the beauty in life and people. I looked for lightness and laughter.

I continue to use this message of Pure Acceptance over and over in my life as a way of letting go, being present, practicing forgiveness, and releasing my perfectionistic tendencies. It pops into my head when I'm confronted with disappointment or when someone lets me down. It pops up when I'm stuck in traffic or when things aren't going my way. Pure Acceptance—it's a good life motto.

The Universe answered me one more time after the treatment for the lymphoma and before the stem cell transplant, which was another trippy experience that I wasn't expecting. I was complete with the chemo, skinny and bald, walking on the beach in Oregon on a clear crisp day before Christmas. I turned to the waves to take in their strength, and with tears in my eyes, I said out loud this time, "Thank you for sparing my life."

This time in my head I heard the response, *Okay. Now go tell everyone.*

And so I am.

SHE MOVES CLOSER TO LOVING HER STRUGGLES

By Huntress Maxine Thompson

Decades of dysfunction had morphed me into a seemingly powerful warrioress—decked out and strong on the outside, yet whimpering in a dark corner on the inside. Years of yoga made my 5'9" frame strong and lean, but internally I was held together by scar tissue from years of hurt. I was able to hide the scars most of the time, only looking the part of a female warrior and not truly feeling it.

I'd long ago resigned myself to a life of treading water in Purgatory. I felt like Sisyphus, the Greek king, forever cursed to pushing a large boulder up a hill only to have it roll to the bottom just as he neared the top. Life seemed an exercise in futility where I never quite got it right.

Key issues persisted, cycling around annually. Each year I vowed to confront and resolve them; each year I missed the deadline. The same issues orbited around me like my very own solar system. Each issue had its own unique properties. Some were so dense and weighty it was difficult to move past them. Some were so hot they would sear my heart and soul when I got near them, while others were so cold they froze me to numbness. A few were flighty and fleeting with periods of retroactivity that complicated things so much I felt like I was doing the moon walk—a whole lot of leg work but no forward movement.

Somehow, I survived. I had no strong sense of self and became whatever I thought others wanted me to be, even if it meant playing dumb. The dumbing down began in high school because smart, geeky girls were unpopular. I deliberately sabotaged, or downplayed, my wisdom-beyond-my-years, which manifested in poor grades and many bad choices. At least I graduated. I considered dropping out in 11th grade, but had enough brains to logically deduce that I'd been in school over half my life and that I was just a little over a year away from getting my diploma.

Artistically, I stopped pursuing things I enjoyed, like music and theater, all so people who would not matter in 10 years wouldn't tease me. If only I'd known! I sold myself out and I wanted out. I was a victim, held hostage by my fears, lack of self and self-worth, and harboring a deep self-loathing.

When I discovered beer, I discovered liquid courage. It numbed me to my weaknesses. It numbed me to the negativity that I soaked in as a Highly Sensitive Person. (I was emo before emo was called "emo"!) Beer shattered my protective shell and gave me the social *cajonés* to at least *attempt* to mix with other people. It usually backfired because of my intolerance to massive amounts of alcohol. When sober, my natural inclination was to be at home: quiet, pensive, and pondering the possibilities in the Universe in my journal or reading books by authors who did the same. I realized being around crowds drained me as I tripped over my social awkwardness. I sucked at small talk; I didn't fit into any group. Though I survived, I was living way below my potential. It was manageable mediocrity.

In recent years, my husband and I had drifted so far apart we were like roommates living completely separate lives under the same roof. We talked *at* each other and not *with* each other, often not even about the same subject. We never slowed down to look each other in the eyes. He stopped asking if his potential plans interfered with any of my plans. He went on a lot of weekend bike events with mixed company; namely with a girl who was obviously and pathetically love sick for him. At times, I practically begged him to stay home and spend time with me. I'd plummeted to the bottom of his priority list.

Around my 50th birthday, I was diagnosed with Hepatitis C. I would need six months of non-radiation chemotherapy. The treatment was brutal and nearly killed me. During those six months, I was a human pincushion, having weekly blood draws to monitor my deteriorating body. My particular chemo, black-boxed by the United States Food and Drug Administration (FDA), was a combination of peg-interferon injections I gave myself once weekly, and daily Ribavirin® pills. The medications drained the life from me. I was teetering on the edge of needing a blood transfusion because of severe anemia. My potassium levels plunged, threatening my central nervous system. My hair fell out so much it was easier to shave it all off, which I did on my husband's 60th birthday while he was away on a 10-day rafting trip that took him off the grid for the duration. When he returned, shocked at the sight of me, he accused me of shaving my head "for attention."

For the most part, it was all I could do to get through the minimal day-to-day activities, which boiled down to medicating myself with that chemo poison and caring for my clowder of kitties. There were days I was so weak and winded I crawled around the house. At my lowest point, only 106 pounds held up my bony 5'9" frame. But taking care of the kitties gave me a reason to live when I otherwise had none. I say that with all seriousness; I honestly wanted out of this body. But I couldn't abandon the kitties and leave them to be gathered up and dispatched to the high-kill house-of-death animal shelter in our small town. They were there when I needed them, with real love, licking my tears, purring in my lap, and lulling me to sleep with their sweet calmness.

The daily Ribavirin® had an opposite effect. It unleashed an angsty side to me that became more of an internal thrashing than an external one. Everything was splayed open, exposing every shred of deeply embedded dysfunction in my psyche. Nothing was sugarcoated. I stood face-to-face with things I'd repressed my whole life — things that were so difficult to look at, it shook me to my core. It all needed releasing and I had to be completely honest with myself while attempting to peel off the layers of dysfunction. But between the drain of the injections and the rage of the pills, I couldn't tell if I was coming or going, or to where, or why. It was a crash course in my personal shadow work that is finally, only now, near completion.

As I dove deeper into treatment, my husband became even more distant. He came by the house only to get the mail and swap out clothing for work or play; I never knew which. Sometimes I got the feeling he came by only to see if I was still alive, hoping I wouldn't be. He treated me with disgust, repulsed by the sight of me. It was such a demeaning charade I finally asked him to stay at our other house, a bad investment he had yet to liquidate. He didn't hesitate and jumped at the chance. He could then go guilt-free on his extended mini-vacations. And he wouldn't be forced to feign concern for me, which he was getting very bad at doing, anyway. It was a most humbling nightmare. I had no strength to even cry or to lash out. Emotionally, I was dead.

During chemo, I managed to blog a little and keep in touch with remote friends on social network sites. Though my body was weak, my mind raged. And then there was Facebook. Finding racy party pictures of some drunken river float event my husband posted was the straw that broke my brittle bones. It was like a slap in the face, though I don't think he intended on me finding those pictures or learning of the event. The pictures were full of fake-breasted, bikini-clad girls his daughter's age posing with props while obviously drunk. On a "strong" day—usually one or two days before my next weekly injection—I mustered the strength to move his belongings to the other house while he was gone. I changed the locks. I secured a lawyer. And he was served.

More than a year later, my clowder of cats and I moved hours away to a new home in a new city. Almost four years after the move and three major foot surgeries later, I'm living alimony to alimony. Rebuilding has been a slow process, especially since my resolve is to overcome my fears and misjudgments about myself *for real* this time and with lasting effect. I had allowed myself to be victimized my entire life because I thought my true self was not worthy or lovable enough. I am still not quite sure *who* I really am. In my decades of dysfunction, I lost all sense of self and am now tasked with putting my Humpty Dumpty Self back together again. I'm 55 going on 18, clueless and directionless.

As far back as I can remember, I said I never wanted to be one of those people who had to have a major tragedy in their lives to shock them awake. I had always hoped I would find myself before a tragic jolt destroyed my little house of cards built on sand. I read a lot of prestigious works on Universal thought by such gurus as Carolyn Myss, Oprah Winfrey, Deepak Chopra, Louise Hay, Wayne Dyer, Eckhart Tolle, Scott Cunningham, Carl Jung, Albert Einstein and Nikola Tesla. I gratefully received refreshing perspectives from lesser known gurus such as Hibiscus Moon, Christine Hassler, and Tess Whitehurst.

The consensus from these teachers is that a major jolt is precisely what is needed in some cases to set a person onto the path of growth and enlightenment. Basically, our egos need to be sent to the proverbial corner to wait in the time-out box while our souls retrieve the almost unrecognizable fragments of our true selves. I now fully accept that energy follows thought and I create my own reality. The road to Self is arduous and the work constant —hourly, daily, weekly, monthly, yearly, and so on.

Though I can't say I've reached nirvana just yet, five years after my dance in hell, I can say I'm on the up side of these excruciating growing pains. The startling discovery was how deeply ingrained the fear, self-loathing, and lack of worth dwelled within me. It disguised itself so well, only revealing itself subtly through my poor choices in men and my lack of confidence not to take on challenges worthy of me. I've also learned that there are no mistakes, only lessons. I maintain an awkward friendship with my estranged husband because I know we were brought together to teach each other something, if only forgiveness.

Some days are better than others, but the gain is worth the struggle. As Carolyn Myss says: "The other side of 'victim' is 'victorious'!" I'm slowly, but surely, replacing my house of cards with a beautiful marble mansion built on a solid foundation.

Through meditation I've learned to slow down my ever-chattering mind enough to know that I am an important part of the whole. We *all* are! I set my intention to grow each day. I think of all the reasons I have to be grateful and to regularly accentuate the positive. I've embraced my introverted nature. I'm at peace with my own company. I no longer feel obligated to let toxic environments and people invade my body or poison my mind. I no longer let people try to squash my flame or kill my light.

But most of all, I'm learning to accept myself fully and love that powerful person unconditionally. We're in it together, all of us. And we're *all* worthy of peace and happiness. Never forget that.

SHE DEEPLY CONNECTS
TO HER HEALING POWERS

By Christine Lisio

r. Ninja Bubbles was floating sideways at the top of his tank. I wasn't sure how long he had been that way, but I was pretty sure it couldn't have been more than a few hours. I jiggled the tank; he wiggled his little fins. He wasn't dead yet.

I was consumed with guilt. Guilt for not changing his water in many months. Guilt for not noticing the white spots on his gills. Guilt for not feeding him enough... or rather, not reminding my eight-year-old son Andrew to feed him, the technical owner of the beautiful blue Beta fish. I then felt guilt for every moment I came up short as a mother and wife! I felt terrible that Mr. Ninja Bubbles's life was barely an afterthought in my crazy existence of daily survival.

Motivated partly by compassion, but mostly out of guilt, I remembered that I actually had healing abilities and that I could try to save him. I quickly assessed his physical condition and saw a big white blob on his eye, which was protruding like a big bubble. The only other thing I could identify were the white spots on his gills. From my healing practices and knowledge, I assessed that it was likely an infection of some sort. I set to work.

When I intuitively tuned in, I found the frequencies of negative bacteria and fungus in his little fish body. He was full of toxins from the infections and the toxic water he was living in. I appealed to the Master Healing Angels, with whom I have the Divine honor and privilege to work with, and invoked the appropriate healing frequencies to kill the infections in his tiny body. All I could do after the healing session was wait and see what happened.

Andrew came into the kitchen where we keep the fish and I pointed out that Mr. Ninja Bubbles was sick. He looked in the tank to check him out and was saddened by the fish's condition, but his face brightened after I told him that I had done some healing work for him. I looked up the life span of Beta fish and prepared my son for the possibility that it could be Mr. Ninja Bubbles time to move on from this existence. We both agreed that whatever happened would be for the highest good.

The next morning, I went about my day completely forgetting about my tiny aquatic patient. I remembered our little fish friend later in the afternoon and quickly went to check on him. What I saw was truly miraculous! His eye had returned to normal size and a healthy condition with the exception of a tiny bit of white on the rim. His gills looked much better and the white spots had shrunk. The most amazing part was that he was no longer floating sideways in his tank; he was swimming around, looking lively. I could not believe my eyes! At this point, I had not been working with the Master

Healing Angels for that long and even though I had had powerful evidence of being able to invoke healing for humans, it was all too easy to doubt my abilities.

When my son returned home from school that day, I had him check out Mr. Ninja Bubbles right away. I said, "Look! Can you believe it? The Master Healing Angels healed him!"

Andrew was beaming as he observed his fish and replied, "Mom, I never doubted the Master Healing Angels."

As if a bolt of lightning dropped down into my head from above, I was stunned by the stark contrast between my eight-year-old's sweet faith, and my own doubts and lack of trust.

It took a little boy and a dying fish to wake me up to the reality that I couldn't see before: I was not standing in my power as a healer. I had been allowing negative thoughts and negative programming to run my life. It was not that I was doubting the power of Master Healing Angels. Rather, I was doubting my worthiness to have them show up for *me*. I was doubting that I have what it takes to instigate healing for a living being, which has been a significant obstacle in moving forward with my own healing and fulfilling my calling as a healer.

In my personal life, I had been working through a difficult long-term chronic illness over the span of ten years. My own healing has been inconsistent for years. It was up. It was down. Oftentimes, it was upside down. All of my physical symptoms had gotten worse recently and, as a result, I was in a very low place emotionally, feeling like I was once again falling into the abyss. So witnessing this undeniable, night-and-day change in the health of our fish was life-changing for me because it was affirming of my healing abilities.

I spent the next several days contemplating the question, "Why is it that I can heal a fish who was down to his last breath, but I can't heal myself?"

The answer I heard was: "Because I didn't believe I could."

Hearing this message was the catalyst for a profound unraveling. The obvious next question was "Why don't I believe that I can?" I set off on a deep quest to find the answer to that question. What was holding me back? What was I believing unconsciously about myself that was keeping me from becoming healthy and strong?

I was learning that healing and Divine Grace are based on personal readiness. Personal readiness is achieved when we have learned the lesson we need to learn from the challenge in front of us. Thus, each soul has its own path for its own growth and development. For me, it was important to learn first-hand, in this lifetime, that I have the power to heal myself. I had to understand that looking outside myself for the answers was not going to take me where I desired to go. Once I was able to truly *get it* and integrate that knowing into my being, everything started to shift. Instead of searching the internet for causes and cures of a particular symptom, I began to look within myself for greater trust and faith.

Many of us have heard in spiritual teachings that we create our own reality. Many of us may even believe this is true. But how many people *know* it's true?

Prior to the healing of our family fish, I came to first understand this truth on an intellectual level. I studied the scientific evidence that quantum physics has shown us about how our thoughts create our reality on the physical plane. Now, as a result of my experience with Mr. Ninja Bubbles, the missing components were coming to light; here began the shift from believing this truth to *knowing* this truth. How did I come to know this truth? For me, it all came down to two things: surrender and faith. It wasn't until I began to identify the many ways in which I was in *resistance* and the many ways in which I was *doubting* that I could begin to transform these parts of myself and start creating what I wanted my life to be.

This was the heart of my journey, right there in front of me. This is when I began to see how I was rejecting my body, rejecting myself, rejecting my gifts and talents. Furthermore, I realized that I was disconnecting from Source at the precise time I needed to connect most. I soon came to the realization that if I connected to Source, my Higher Self, and my Guides, I had all the support I needed.

I was now beginning to *know* this concept of "creating my reality" as my truth, and I was able to start using this truth to change my world. I was finally nourishing my body and spirit with the necessary building blocks to heal from within. I was learning how to identify the deepest emotions hidden within me so I could let go of the resistance. I moved from pushing the pain and suffering away from me, to honoring it, embracing it, and healing it. I shifted from *believing* that I could create my own reality to *knowing* it as my truth.

As I moved through this process, my life started to change. I was no longer that chronically-ill mother of two, struggling to keep her head above water. I stepped into my power and Soul purpose as a healer and teacher. Each layer of my own healing journey served to provide me with the growth and insights necessary to make me even better, stronger, and more powerful in my work and my life, evolving into the person I always wanted to be.

I reflect back on that time in my life with awe for the subtle, yet powerful ways that we, as Souls in human form, are guided by the Universe to grow and evolve. I never would have imagined that a little blue Beta fish could be the catalyst for such a pivotal period of growth in my life, but it's all about personal readiness, isn't it? I was ready for transformation, and all I needed was the gentle nudge of an unexpected aquatic teacher to push me forward. I have so much gratitude for Mr. Ninja Bubbles, for being with our family and providing me the opportunity to know myself better.

This turning point in my life was about realizing I have the power to transform my life, to change my reality. And that is exactly what I learned how to do. Once I was able to identify the underlying emotions that were keeping me in a place of resistance, I was able to release the emotions, release the resistance, and transform those parts of me that I wanted to change.

This was a beautiful gift; a transformation that I allowed myself to receive. Moving into the acceptance of *what is,* and releasing the resistance to *what is,* frees up the energy to create something new.

SHE EVOLVES INTO MOTHERHOOD

By Molly McCord

A friend of mine said it best: "Nothing can prepare you for that first week."

Yet I tried my very best regardless, like any pregnant woman with access to multiple resources would do. I researched newborn baby topics on Google; read all of the blog posts on popular motherhood websites; packed the hospital bag early with highly recommended essentials and extras; bought all of the top-rated post-natal care products to help with healing; and inquired with moms and my doctor on anything else that came to mind. The nursery was soon packed with tiny diapers, board books, and bright wooden toys; sweet little onesies and cashmere-soft blankets were stacked and organized in drawers; pre-made dinners were stocked in the freezer. By all appearances, I was as prepared as could be. Not to mention that a new mother's best friend, Amazon Prime, was just an easy click away for any urgent necessities.

As my bump grew with each passing month, I

continued working diligently in my home office as a self-employed entrepreneur. I was seated in front of the computer by 7:30 a.m., hot coffee right next to the mousepad, and highly-focused on the day's tasks as I fired up my fingers on the laptop. My To-Do list was packed with any number of evolving priorities: one-on-one sessions with clients, writing, podcasting, teaching classes, blogging, posting, creating, organizing, filming, or editing. Every day whizzed by with productivity, then I'd break in the afternoon for a walk around the block as my belly became bigger and my body moved slower.

The ninth month hormones really started acting up one summer night while watching television. My bump was full and large under a bowl of disappearing Greek yogurt. I abruptly turned to my husband during a commercial break.

"Someday he's going to get married and leave us." I started blinking faster. Those pregnancy hormones can sure run you through the ringer.

"Let's let him be born first," said the non-pregnant, logical person on the couch.

"I hope his wife is a good one. I know he'll choose a good one." Like I needed more things to worry about at that moment in time.

"Maybe she's not even born yet."

"Well she better hurry up and get here! Tick tock, tick tock!" Probably too soon to open up a Match.com account for him.

Then a little bump of a knee — or maybe an elbow — rose on my belly. Cold foods like yogurt seemed to get him moving more, and in a few minutes he'd probably have hiccups again. I loved this little one so much already. Yes, my unborn son would certainly move out of the house at some point, but right now, he was all mine, warm and snug in my belly.

I jokingly called this my "geriatric pregnancy" because, after passing the ripe old age of 38, common medical information considered it nearly time to park my ancient uterus in the junkyard. It was reassuring, however, for my obstetrician to share that most of her pregnant patients were in the 35- to 40-year-old age bracket these days. Phew, I wasn't the only fully occupied geezer uterus in town. And thankfully, my pregnancy was healthy and normal during the whole gestation period. I was energetic and as busy as ever, working all the way up to my last week of pregnancy. I had no plans to give up my work as an entrepreneur even as this next part of my life was just beginning.

I had no idea how everything about my daily world was about to change forever.

Labor began one week early on a Saturday afternoon, which was wonderfully convenient since my husband was home and I did not have to freak out on him over the phone. The first contractions started slowly, making me stop and pause in the hallway as I wondered, *Is this the real thing?* Then they progressively grew more intense and frequent through the evening hours and into the night as the soft moon rose higher and higher in the sky. We waited until the contractions increased according to the 4-1-1 rule (occurring 4 minutes apart, lasting for 1 minute, for 1 hour), and then when the sun started to peek over the horizon, we finally left for the hospital at 5 a.m.

Five hours later, I had an emergency Caesarian section because my sweet little baby boy was not getting enough oxygen into his sweet little baby body. Thankfully, he arrived very strong, healthy, and hungry. My husband and I drove away from the hospital with our newborn in the typical state of new parent fog: exhaustion, relief, trepidation, joy, and in full protective mode.

It turned out, my friend was 100% right: Nothing prepared us for that first week of parenthood at home. I was awake every two or three hours to feed my ravenous son, which meant never sleeping deep enough at one time. My husband and I shared duties as best we could, making us both physically, emotionally, and mentally wiped out beyond anything we had known before. The rolling exhaustion never ceased, and all we could do was ebb and flow with the waves of this new lifestyle. It was the most tortured we'd ever felt, combined with the elation of holding and nurturing our newborn.

The first month at home with my son was quiet as I spent days sitting on the couch feeding him, holding him, watching him sleep peacefully, and allowing my body to heal from major surgery. Binge-watching television was my new daily routine as the exhaustion continued. Being able to nap while he slept was a welcomed respite, although not as easy as I'd thought it would be. Any day with a quick shower was considered a winning day.

The love I felt for this little precious one was beyond description. His sweet toes, tiny fingernails, and growing hair were so charming to witness. He was inquisitive and engaging, and there was nothing more heartwarming than feeling his baby body nestled against my chest for comfort and warmth.

Yet as the months passed, I also found myself in a deep well of struggle with this new daily experience. I was barely functioning with so little sleep. My body was healing slowly. The days were filled with boredom, silence, monotony. I was not made for child care around the clock, I told myself. I could not be a full-time mom and completely give up my work, I told myself. I could not see an end in sight. I did not know how to move through this deep maternal need to care for this new life, when at the same time, it seemed like an integral part of myself was fading away.

I would slowly shuffle past my shut-down office, bleary-eyed, and could faintly see the Ghost of My Former Self: sitting at the desk, typing, creating, concentrating, clicking away contently. She was intense and focused; adept at completing a minimum of three things on her To Do list every day. She was in control, active, inspired, and well-rested.

Then in a soft blink, this Ghost of My Former Self coasted away as I was brought back to my new reality of very little sleep, ongoing physical exhaustion, emotional confusion, and uncertainty about the path ahead.

For all of the gratitude I felt for having this perfect baby, I did not expect to feel a loss for my former self and previous daily reality. Maybe other new moms were better at full-time child care and could make this transition with more grace. Maybe other new moms "got their bodies back" in only a few months. Maybe other new moms were more mentally prepared for this big change. Maybe other new moms felt it was a smoother life transition, or easier to switch to being an around-the-clock milk-mamma, or maybe they welcomed insta-baby life more quickly.

I was not that new mama. I was horribly messy, wildly unprepared, and extremely hard on myself. Not to mention, the post-pregnancy hormones only made the highs and lows more dramatic as it felt like I was riding on a giant emotional swing for one. Grace was definitely *not* my middle name.

The push-and-pull between career and family was officially a real dilemma that I now understood beyond simple Facebook memes or trendy blog posts. I was woefully unprepared for the frustration I would feel over the lack of satisfying creative days. I even resented my husband's ability to leave the house, drive in a car by himself, and be in an adult workplace—and I told him so. I was fully committed to being a mother, but I still needed mental stimulation, creative expression, and productive satisfaction.

And there was absolutely no freakin' way I would give up this precious little one that I was holding for anything else, even when I missed the Ghost of My Former Self. I knew this phase simply came down to allowing more time to adjust to this new normal and being willing to surrender to *what is* without missing the present moment.

So I finally allowed the Ghost of My Former Self to softly disappear. I did not need her around anymore to hold up my former world, old priorities, or the previous version of life that no longer existed. I now knew I would never work as fast as she did, or have time to concentrate for hours, or accomplish in a day what she could. She was a beautiful version of that life—and she really rocked it.

But now there was a new Boss in town for this work-at-home mama, and he kept me on my toes like no other Boss I've had before. My new daily routine involves stopping everything I am doing to go outside and watch the always-fascinating garbage trucks move through our neighborhood. I can work on the computer for probably an hour while Sesame Street sings, counts, dances, and plays on the television. When a sippy cup is missing, we stop everything to look in the bathtub first; a bottom dresser drawer second. There will be a loud demand for crackers, cheese, and milk right in the middle of Target, which will then get louder as I try to keep the strong-willed toddler sitting his little bum down in the shopping cart.

Just kidding. Those are other people's kids.

Later, we'll go to the park before it gets too hot, and push trucks in between the couch cushions, and he'll throw chicken bits on the floor because they are not crackers, and then it will be nap time. I will use those hours to turn my focus back to my business, where I have adjusted my expectations of myself wildly. The next project will launch later than I originally planned. The other five books I am working on will sit for a while (and then longer). My next class will be taught a month later. I will only film business videos on a Saturday morning when my husband is home. I won't post to Facebook as often as before. I will respond to emails later rather than sooner.

And it will all be okay. In fact, it will be better than okay because there is more joy, trust, laughter, and playtime on this path than the Ghost of My Former Self could ever imagine. I am only two years in to this grand Mother of a journey and I'm still figuring it out each day as a work-at-home entrepreneur. I anticipate that will never change, truthfully.

As I type these words, the Boss just found me sitting here on the floor trying to finish this essay. There's a sippy cup swinging in one hand; a bright book dangling in the other. He's strutting this way, giant blue eyes fixed on my lap. In a matter of seconds, he'll walk up to my feet, stepping on them as he turns around, and then sit himself down right inside my crossed legs. He'll officially hand me the book, drop the sippy cup, then cross his ankles and recline into my chest. We'll read the big bright book at least twice—unless we hear a garbage truck outside.

Best thing ever. Perhaps modern work-at-home motherhood is simply the evolution that continually redefines what we call the *best thing ever*. I believe we are meant to transform our self-definitions into more expanded views and wider understandings as we evolve from girls, to teenagers, to young adults, to women, to wise crones—and a thousand more phases of Self along the way.

Among other things, I hope I am teaching him the joy of finding a job that you're passionate about, the satisfaction of being creatively and mentally engaged in daily life, and the importance of "no touch" when his fingers want to pound on my keyboard as I respond to an email. Among other things, he is teaching me that changing a diaper always outweighs opening an urgent email, closing down my laptop is actually incredibly liberating, and chasing squirrels is more memorable than gaining social media followers. Some days, neither of us get what we want, be it making headway on a project or making big milk puddles on the kitchen floor.

Gratefully, I have learned that you do not have to be thoroughly prepared for all of life's changes. Instead, you just need to stay open to how life can change you.

One day, he will move out and find his life partner (who might, or might not, be born yet) and get married and understand that we're not going to decorate the chairs with yogurt this morning. Until then, we will crawl, walk, and run together as mutual teachers through the continual release, and gain, of life's priorities.

SHE CONNECTS

{ Soul Mates and Relationships }

"She loves herself enough to show up and listen to her guidance, her Soul's whispers. Living authentically with brutal self-honesty is a commitment she has made to herself numerous times throughout the journey. She recommits to both her inner knowingness and her trust in something bigger than herself. *She's got this.*"

The Modern Heroine's Journey of Consciousness

SHE BLOOMS WITH WISDOM
FROM A FRIENDSHIP'S END

By Sharon Bright

As we walked out of the café that morning, we were hopeful. The sun was even shining on an English winter's day. Or maybe that is just how I remember it because I wanted the cloud over our friendship to fade. We had been uncomfortable with each other for months. In our attempt to talk through everything that morning, I had promised her I was not like others from her past and that I would not leave her. I meant it. I desperately wanted her to believe me when I looked into her eyes and said it. We hugged before we left and she told me she loved me. We were hopeful.

I drove away with a sinking feeling in my stomach that meant we were still not right. It was undeniable, even though all I wanted was to feel joy, relief, something other than the truth. By the time I pulled into my driveway, I knew our friendship would never be as it was before.

In the house, I sat at the dining room table to process

what had happened. I remember repeatedly thinking that my friend was broken somehow, and I did not know how to fix the pain for her. When she stopped smiling, long enough for me to see her pain, there was more there than I could help. I had spent months thinking that our previous miscommunications would blow over and I could prove to her that our friendship could outlast petty feuds. That day, however, I understood the depths of what we both brought to the table; past hurts lingered in us, established well before we ever met.

When the friendship was good, she made me laugh. We explored simple findings: a quaint pub stop for lunch, or driving through the rolling English countryside for antiques. We were happy to continue along the same road, travelling and filling our cars with treasures. However, life is not about staying the same. Instead, it is a constant classroom trying to teach us to push past the familiar. In order to grow, we must be willing to face discomforts, as we also find joy.

I knew that she periodically had emotional times that would overtake her. Having gone through my own personal traumas, I began to feel an intuitive need to open up to her more. There is profound encouragement when a friend takes your hand through troubles. Admitting your vulnerabilities takes courage. You have to trust that the other person will be there for you no matter what you reveal. We were missing that trust and no shopping adventure in the world would find it. We had reached a crossroads. Either she could trust me with her sadness, truth, and fears, or I had to trust that a friendship without such depth would not work for me.

When the first signs of mistrust seeped into our friendship, I tried to stop it. I guarded against it by being more available to her. I did not want to lose what we had invested. I was trying my best to hold back a broken dam, my arms outstretched, all the while denying that I was drenched. The seeping became full-on leaks, and then finally a flood. Nothing was holding back this lesson that life wanted for us. Nothing I said was going to keep her in my life. Like mirrors, we reflected each other's core inability to present our whole selves in a friendship, broken parts and all. With that realization, I knew I needed to learn to trust myself and to believe in myself more, no matter how hard it might be. Though it broke my heart, I began the journey that meant losing her friendship, and ultimately, befriending myself.

I took a long walk after our final goodbye. Six months on from the café day, she was moving away from England. Those six months had put me through hell. I felt judged. I felt disliked. I felt wrong. I felt bad. The walk was an attempt to blow away my heartache. I lived only a neighborhood stroll from Stonehenge, so I set out towards the monument, hoping that its mystical healing qualities could provide some clarity. I planned to walk until all my painful thoughts made some sense.

Halfway between my house and the stones, between steps and tears, I clearly heard the message: *Sometimes in your absence, you can teach someone more.*

Then I understood. She and I were meant to be in each other's lives for only moments. Without the willingness to go deeper as friends, we restricted the advancement of our inner wisdom. Our souls had agreed that the potential for our individual growth would far outweigh the friendship ending.

Her absence would teach me. My absence would teach her. By letting her go, life was giving me an invitation to meet my inner self more deeply. I reflected on what I wanted for my life and in my close relationships. I knew I could no longer deny parts of myself or compromise my need to maintain a friendship. Our relationship would become a beautiful lesson lifting me out of both the self-criticisms and comfort zones to which I had become accustomed. My hope was that she would accept the invitation for soul growth, too. Possibly, she would look back one day and see that I really did love her. If this was supposed to heal and create a higher version of each of us, I was willing to be the one who decided never to speak to her again. I was oh so very hopeful.

Then she was gone for good.

Our friendship went on to become an onion of lessons for me. I peeled back layer upon layer revealing what I had missed before. I had a few people in my life who would lovingly allow me to hash out the details. I was adamant that I was not going to turn our friendship into some vicious cycle of gossip. I kept my peace and only trusted my story to those who would appreciate my need to see all of their perspectives. With their support, I experimented with being my most authentic self. I shared my fears, my interests, my beliefs, and my passions. I described my heartache and my emotional triggers. I slowly regained my confidence in friendships. I leaned more into those relationships that accepted me fully. I knew that I could never let another person cloud what I knew about myself again. I started to trust myself, and from that, I deepened my trust in others.

One of those friends, a guide who patiently dissected the whole terrible ordeal with me, once said, "I think you would have eventually become bored within the friendship." I knew she was right. I had been suppressing vital parts of me in order to be liked.

When you are not putting your whole self into a

relationship, you are wearing a mask. Actually, in the beginning of every relationship, we wear masks for protection. As time goes on, you try to reveal more and more of your core self. When the other person meets these parts of you with interest, the mask slips away. For a while, though, the mask remains close to your side as a safety measure. You could easily slip it back on if you ever felt rejected or hurt by another. Many masks we wear carry a huge smile, even though they hide a stream of tears. I learned that I had worn my mask too often in that friendship. The performance would have become tiresome and boring over time because a mask could not be permanent. It does not represent the complete you that you are put in this life to be.

When I took off my mask and dove into the center of my being, I found that there were standards in friendships I had forgotten. I needed to be able to be imperfect, to say the wrong thing from time to time, and be forgiven when I said I was sorry. I needed to talk about what was on my mind; not just the cheerful stuff, but also the dark, murky, confusing parts of me that wanted acceptance. I needed to be there for a friend in a way that made me feel inspiring and purposeful. I needed to have my personal boundaries around my time and energy respected and supported. I needed the space to have more than one friend so I could benefit from understanding all the parts of me I discovered in their beautiful reflections.

I had not safeguarded those fundamental needs. I had, unfortunately, allowed my intentions to be swayed according to someone else's perception of me. I had broken my own heart. I was not there for me. I had left myself, even while I had promised another I would never leave them. I began to understand how important being myself was if I was going to succeed in having friendships that had the connection I craved.

And like magic, the more I put my authenticity out to the external world, gorgeous people remained, came back and showed up in my life to support me. My tribe grew larger. They loved me without me having to do anything for them. My presence was enough.

Thich Nhat Hanh, the world-renowned Buddhist monk says, "Love in such a way that the other person feels free." The magic in that wisdom is that you develop a genuine need to do for others when you are free from the obligation of their expectations of you. I was meant to be free, and in so doing, learn to love others with a freedom so fierce that if they really needed to leave my life for the pursuit of their own path, I could understand.

I realized that everything in my past was perfectly orchestrated to bring me to this point on my journey. I was always meant to come out from behind the scared girl that was afraid someone might not like her. The girl that would mold herself around another's needs, instead of her own, all in thinking that was good friendship.

And then I was back for good.

I laughed with a friend recently as I realized that this onion of a friendship was the size of a cabbage now. The never-ending layers and lessons had permeated so many parts of my life! The French use "mon petit chou," literally "my little cabbage," as a term of endearment. That is how I felt about the friendship. It had expanded from an onion to a cabbage-size lesson because it brought me to some perspectives about my past, my purpose, and my healing that I needed to fully comprehend. I was able to see my relationships with not just other friends, but also my husband, my children, my parents, and my extended family in a fresh way. I more easily held space for people to be whoever they needed to be, which was not dependent on my needs. I became much more confident and knew that it was acceptable to not invite everyone into my life, instead holding them at a distance with love. I was no longer as sensitive to others' opinions of me, as I had been in the past. I clearly understood that all relationships, and their endings, are tools to help us grow into who we are meant to be.

I recently had an epiphany when I reflected on words that my former friend had shared with me about her emotional struggles and how she felt she did not add value to those around her at times. It was one of the few small windows into her soul that she cautiously allowed me to see, and I felt fortunate she did. If she had not, I would not have been able to attest to how her presence in my life was invaluable to my journey to find more of myself. I hope that one day she may realize that, and know my gratitude for our short friendship. I remain so very hopeful.

SHE DANCES HER WAY BACK TO HAPPINESS

By Lili Krnic

Divorce. The word itself feels heavy and final and acidic, just as the process tends to be. It's the end of love, the end of trying, the end of hope. The loss of hope is always the hardest for an eternal optimist. Hope is what propels us forward in life; a driving energy that gets us through the challenging times. It's only when hope finally dies that we have nothing left to justify our unhappiness.

One hot January night, while in one of my favorite places in the world, my hope was extinguished. On vacation to rekindle our strained marriage, my husband and I had every reason to be happy and relaxed: we were child-free for the trip and surrounded by the lushest, most vibrant examples of nature to be found. Families of monkeys were swinging in plain sight, iguanas scurried in all directions, jewel-toned butterflies floated above our heads, and the ocean was visible in the distance. This backdrop was one I had longed for since the last time I had been to Central America three years earlier. It was the one place that made me feel most alive when, for the most part, I was feeling increasingly dead inside.

I was a wife, mother, teacher, and business owner, but as each of these roles increased in scope, I lost more and more of myself. It didn't help that I was married to a man who didn't understand the meaning of true partnership and lived his life with no regard for my thoughts or feelings. It didn't help that I was essentially a single mother cloaked in the disguise of a healthy marriage, waiting patiently for the day when my marriage would morph into that beautiful, loving, respectful union that my heart longed for.

I would regularly talk myself out of this longing because I tried to convince myself that such relationships didn't exist or that I was just too demanding. Tone down your expectations. Want less. Be happy with what you've got. Look at the positive. Don't complain. No marriage is perfect. Ignore the ache in your heart. Toughen up and dry your tears. Think of the kids. Maybe you're the problem. Work on yourself. Go back to therapy. Read another self-help book. In any case, these messages were also what my husband continuously told me, and I had started to believe them.

I had been steadfast in my devotion to the marriage despite the constant negation from my husband. As each year passed, and increasingly since the birth of our children, there was less and less room allowed for me. I was saddled with all of the childcare responsibilities and most of the work related to the upkeep of our home, as well as our nourishing. My husband found many excuses to be busy. And if there was ever a hint of resentment from me because he was not available *yet one more* evening, there would be the trusted reason that he was busy with something work-related.

My frustration mounted as I spent month after month playing both mommy and daddy to our boys. If I had received some level of appreciation or support it could have been tolerable, but instead, I was expected to lavishly appreciate my husband's efforts, even when they moved our family backwards.

I swam in this mess of emotions for years, gradually feeling the heavier and heavier burden of caring for both of our sons, and the responsibility for business ventures I didn't choose. Despite my clear opposition to the idea, my husband had decided to use a chunk of our money to fund the opening of a bakery, ignoring the fact that he had no experience or knowledge of the field. Soon I found myself running a shop selling the very things I previously counseled people to avoid eating. My integrity was stretched to its edge.

However, marriage is such that unless you are prepared to divorce, you are forced to accept and deal with every decision—good or bad—that your partner makes. And my husband leveraged the fact that he knew I wasn't going anywhere. Dismissive of my concerns, he would often taunt me by saying, "If you don't like things, go back and live with your mother," knowing this was a worse alternative for me than staying with him.

But that day in January, in my real world paradise, as I sat in our beautiful glass-crafted boutique hotel room, I got pushed to a limit that I didn't even know existed. Finally, with time to talk and no distractions of children or work, I pressed him to answer the questions about our finances that he never wanted to address back home.

"How much of our money have you spent?" I asked.

Silence. Always silence from him. It was an avoidance tactic I had grown to loathe. My instincts told me the answer was bad.

It turned out he had spent all of the money from the recent sale of our home. As a mother of two small children who had already turned the corner on forty, I was gutted. My past and my future both disappeared with that revelation of financial loss as the relationship I had cultivated for 12 years crumbled before my eyes, taking with it all of my expectations of security for the years ahead. In that moment, it became very clear that I could no longer continue being an accomplice in my own annihilation.

That night, I sobbed and screamed like I never had before, and prayed never to again. In that glass room, a fishbowl with little more than sheer white curtains shielding me from the next guests mere six feet away, I was finally done. All lingering hope was completely sucked out of me.

I cried so hard I made myself sick. Saying I was actually sick was a convenient excuse for the red eyes and the runny nose that the hotel staff considerately inquired about. It helped explain the sullen look on my face as I quickly passed the happy, honeymooning couples with their shining eyes. I couldn't eat and I could barely drink. My body went into such shock that I didn't move my bowels for eight days. By the time I finally did, the pain was as bad as childbirth. It was insult added to injury — God's cruel joke, I thought.

I spent much of that trip on the cold, cement bathroom floor because it was the only flat space in our room besides the bed. He got the bed. He always did. And while I grieved my life as I knew it — my marriage, my family, my future — he watched action movies on his laptop. Occasionally he would look at me with the same detachment with which he watched his movies. I kept waiting for — hoping for — some emotion, but nothing came. It didn't seem possible that we were sharing the same reality.

I had had so many small reasons to leave my husband before that, but not one that I believed was big enough. If I had piled up all the small reasons, one on top of the other, I would have been able to see a valid excuse to leave. But when you obligate yourself to look on the bright side and to persevere for love and family, you train yourself to forgive and forget regularly, sometimes daily, evenly hourly.

Divorcing was hard. Very hard. Perhaps the hardest thing I've ever had to do. Leaving behind 12 years of a life built with a spouse, and a family- no matter how fractured — was the impossible decision that I eventually made. If I wasn't going to listen to all the smaller warnings life was continuously presenting to me, I would have to finally pay attention to the big one — that there wasn't room in my marriage for two equals, only one inflated ego. And it was with that ultimate example of selfishness and disrespect that I finally had my "big enough" reason; I finally felt justified in my decision to leave.

In the following months, I grieved for my marriage and the loss of my intact nuclear family. With the help of a therapist, I came to understand that what I grieved for the most was the loss of my *dream* of a marriage and a family, since the reality was not at all what I had envisioned. Letting go of all the hopes for what could have been was ultimately what eased my suffering. Once I was able to let go of the fantasy that I had carried with me for so long, it was easier to put my focus where it should be: on rebuilding my life in such a way that I could be the best mother for my sons and the best version of myself for everyone else, especially me.

Having been so busy with all the responsibilities that had been piled on me while married, I hadn't had time to come up for air for a very long time. I had had very little time for anything that was important to my own growth and happiness. So during the times that my sons were with their father, I began to do things that nourished my spirit and allowed me to remember why life was worth living.

I realized dance was one of the few things that made me feel better while I was dealing with so much despair. So when my friends asked me what I wanted to do for my birthday, I told them I wanted to go dancing. And we did. We put on our sneakers and went to a club filled with people almost half our age, and we danced. I danced until I could feel the smile return to my face. And I knew I had to keep dancing.

I continued to go dancing with my girlfriends to places where I could lose myself in crowds, and strangers began commenting on how happy I looked. I went to Zumba class and moved my hips in ways that I had never felt free to do in any other space. I went to Ecstatic Dance where I moved my way through emotions that my body was desperate to release. Eventually I danced my way back to the me that I knew was still there, buried under years of unhappiness and sacrifice, the *me* that took pleasure in feeling the rhythm in my body and the joy from expressing that rhythm in my own way. When I danced, I was ageless and problem-free. Dancing was my medicine, my meditation, my prayer. When I danced, I was in that rare space where I was happy to be me again.

Almost immediately, dancing began to change and heal me in a way I couldn't foresee. By allowing myself to do what I loved to do, my days began to feel lighter and I began to feel more optimistic. And with that optimism came a flow and ease that I hadn't anticipated. Things in my life began working out. I managed to buy a house with very little to my name and despite a thousand obstacles. I was thriving at a new job in a new field that I loved. I eventually began to date some fabulous men and I even found myself enjoying being single. After about a year, I attracted an incredible man into my life who I adore and who adores me. I am grateful every day for how easy and open our relationship is.

Today, I live my life differently than I ever have. I don't continuously sacrifice all my needs and desires so that others can be comfortable. I play full out in my life and I regularly make space for the things that bring me joy, whether it's dance, travel, art, or the appreciation of beauty.

Once upon a time, I believed that I needed to set aside my own happiness in order to increase that of another's. Now I realize that my happiness adds to the lives of others. The world doesn't need more unhappy people trying to do the right thing; it needs more laughter and smiles, as do my children. This is the legacy I aspire to leave—a life lived in the pursuit of love, joy, and the happy, hopeful possibility of being fully alive.

SHE REKINDLES HER FIRE WITHIN

By Diana "Dynasty" Hardy

"I know it seems strange, right?
I'm full grown but I feel like a kid like…
I've got so much to learn.
Touch the fire just to see if it burns…
yea, I know it absurd.
'Cause by this time I should know better…"

I paused to acknowledge a simple truth: *Where I am is a direct result of my actions.*

This is where my own lyrics revealed something to me that made me sit up straight in my chair.

Did I get burned by a love flame…again?

I mean, have you ever seen a fire show? It is beautiful. The light is magnetizing and captivating. Ever been to a hibachi joint? Everybody is all "ooooh" and "ahhhh" while trying to avoid having their eyelashes singed off. There is something about the beauty of the flame that draws you close; oftentimes, closer than you should be.

Yet I was flat out tired from being a citizen of the world and having my heart burned again. Had I been behaving poorly?

The previous summer, I was on the beach underneath a gigantic ball of fire, becoming more and more bronze by the minute. Laying with my eyes closed, taking in the sounds of the waves, occasionally walking out into the Gulf as far as I could without fear of being swept away. I stood there staring into the vastness. I felt so small. Humbled. "Wow," I thought, "This world is so huge." Feeling the water all around and seeing tiny fish swimming around my feet, my mind shifted to my vast possibilities. I felt full of opportunity. I affirmed myself in that water and set the intention to live more consciously. When it was time to pack up and leave the beach, I felt ready for the world.

The following months were incredible. I quit the corporate job I'd had for more than six years. I committed to things that were in alignment with my vision: serving youth, teaching middle school, performing more. I loved it! Then I met a guy. (There's always a guy.) He had his own thing going on and he was a ton of fun to be around. Best of all, I was loving ME, grandly. Many of the intentions that I'd set at the beach were manifesting and I was so excited. "Ahhh," I thought, "THIS is the LIFE! I am on my way to exactly where I want to be!"

Then, things started changing. Engulfed in this new relationship, I became distracted. I was consumed by this new flame. He wasn't really my boyfriend, but my heart didn't know that. This is often the recipe for disaster — giving commitment-level experiences to someone with whom you have no commitment. So many people talk about giving of yourself with no expectations, and sometimes I envy them. How...do...you...do...it?

My relationship philosophy is something like this: I like you, you like me, we're a couple. Ha! This is totally contrary to the way things go these days. Somehow society has convinced many of us that love is not where it's at and that we should fight like hell to maintain our independence and not "catch feelings." Well, this girl catches feelings. I caught them so hard that when this whirlwind romance was over, my head was left spinning. He had to move away for work and had no desire to continue this "thing" that we had. Suddenly, the woman who stood on the beach, feeling full of opportunity, greatness and power was nowhere to be found.

Where had she gone?

That woman was confident, ready to conquer the world. That woman saw greatness in herself. She was intentional and unwilling to settle. Amazed by the magnificence of the sun, he had seen the light in herself.

But after this relationship ended, I somehow managed to forget these things, and found myself captivated by smaller sparks that should not have been fanned. Even when we are full grown and we know that fire is dangerous, we are still fascinated by the flame.

So I went back to the beach. I looked out onto the vastness of the ocean. I again felt so small, so humbled. I sat down at the shore and let the water wash over my feet. I reflected over the past year, the incredible joys, the heartaches, the wins, and the losses. I considered my role in each part. I wasn't behaving poorly. I was just out of alignment with my true self. I'd abandoned my intentions. The truth was that I'd known that these relationships weren't the best for me, but believing that I needed something outside of myself, I'd allowed them to happen. That day I recommitted to myself at the shore. No more settling. If having the love that I desired meant waiting, then I'd wait. To be able to do the type of work that I love, I'd apply myself more. I would step into the heat that was outside of my comfort zone. And I did.

I rekindled the fire within. I walked away from anything that wasn't good for my soul. If it didn't contribute to my overall well-being, it wasn't for me. I remembered that there were people who were waiting for me to show up. I wanted my best life. I prayed more. I ate like I loved myself. I made time for me.

After this recommitment, it seemed as though doors of opportunity were flung open for me. I led my own summer arts program. I created. I connected. I did the work that I am here to do. I rediscovered my light and it was bright! I learned that while fire can sometimes burn you, it can also save you.

It's the fire that warms you when life gets cold.

It's the fire that illuminates your soul to shine bright for the world to see.

Magnetizing.

Captivating.

Not for your glory, but to show that when we dare to truly embrace our own light, we are set ablaze.

SHE OPENS HER HEART
AND OWNS HER POWER

By Holly Faith

Throughout my life, my inner strength and power have shown up during all of my hardships. It was so natural that I didn't even know what it was. I was born a survivor and I knew how to get through most anything. At birth, I survived a surgery that only three doctors in the United States knew how to perform. And as a teenager, my parents weren't around so I learned how to survive by going to school and working hard to feed and take care of myself.

It wasn't until later in life that I was truly tested by going through my toughest survival period—the challenges of the heart. I experienced a divorce that left me feeling lost and alone. Soon after, my brother and father died only months apart, leaving me in total darkness and despair. I was living in a place where I didn't have any friends or support. I sunk into deep loneliness. Feeling lost and alone in a dark hole, I wondered how I was going to make it through. It's as though my strength and survivor instincts were fading.

During this time, two relationships really motivated me to make the changes I needed. These were soul mate connections that showed up at the perfect time in my life. They were both with guys I knew from my childhood, so this was the second time they each reappeared in my life.

Tommy and I were reacquainted about eight months after my divorce. I was concentrating on building my business and trying to make friends in my new town. He was fun and made me laugh, as he still acted like the silly 12-year-old boy I knew from way back in the day. Since we didn't live near each other, we went away on adventures together. We hiked, explored new places, and sang out of tune. We were focused on entertainment and enjoying life. Our time together reminded me how to loosen up and get excited about living again.

We fell in love, and a few years later, we decided to move in together. Once we did, our relationship totally changed—it fell apart. I felt like I turned into his mother, having to take care of him. We never laughed and hung out with each other anymore; he just always disappeared. We became distant roommates. I was miserable. I tried talking to him and working on our issues, but he didn't want to put in any effort. When it finally ended and he moved out, I found out he had been cheating on me. Hurt but not surprised, I totally cut him out of my life.

I had had enough. I was tired of heartbreak and ready for a total life overhaul. I knew I needed to change myself in order to change my circumstances. I was ready to explore my deep, dark world so I could heal and transform my life. I hired Rochelle, a transformational coach trained by self-help author and teacher Debbie

Ford. Rochelle has a heart of gold and she truly loves her work. In our weekly sessions, she knew the tough words I needed to hear to get the most out of my coaching. Then I used the rest of the week to process and ask myself the right questions, going deeper inside to find the answers.

I saw how my destructive patterns were created at a very young age. I cried away a lot of the hurt. I identified the stagnant beliefs that didn't ring true to me anymore and I replaced them with new and powerful ones. I was breaking down the barriers that were keeping me hostage from my own happiness. And I learned how to be tender and loving to myself during the entire coaching process.

At the beginning of my coaching, my second soul mate reappeared in my life. Sonny was my high school crush. My heart sang every time I saw him. We never dated as teenagers but we had been friends. His sister, Charlotte, and I were like sisters, and their family felt like my family. So Sonny was 'the brother' and I saw him often at Charlotte's family gatherings. Sometimes it was awkward to be alone with him or look him in the eyes; I was afraid of what feelings might show up.

Interestingly, Sonny and I reconnected at a time when we both needed to be heard. I felt a deep connection with him from the beginning. He intrigued me and I wanted to get to know him more. We were vulnerable with each other in a way we couldn't be with others. We laughed and joked around a lot. There was a deep caring between us that was truly genuine. It really felt good to spend time with him, especially since he encouraged me to stay on track with my coaching sessions.

Not too long after my coaching ended, Sonny and I

parted ways, mostly because he lived almost a thousand miles away and I was moving even farther across the country. I always felt our connection was going to be temporary; I just didn't think it was going to end so soon.

We tried to remain friends, but it was hard. I truly felt the love connection between us and I didn't want that to go away. We would be close and intimate one minute, and the next we were literally miles apart. I wanted more of the heated passion between us and I longed for his kisses. I saw the energetic dance between us and I was unsure of which way I really wanted to go. I missed him most of the time, and, other times, I wanted to free myself from what no longer was.

A few months later, while we were still figuring out how our new friendship was to unfold, I found out he was dating someone else. I was hurt and confused because he hadn't told me there was another person who was special in his life. He and I used to be able to share everything, so I didn't understand why he couldn't share this. His explanation was that he didn't want to hurt me. That really confused me even more because I already knew we were just friends, or so I had been telling myself. After a bitter and agonizing fall out, I was able to defend and express my anger in a way that made me feel better—my power was showing up again. I was respectful yet assertive with him. It was amazing to me how I could express my rage in a way that was clearly understood by the other person. That conversation brought up so much clarity between us. We saw that we both had been hurt and he apologized. I explained what I had learned from our relationship, and we both cried. I felt peaceful and content at last. It was time to let go.

I had felt safe enough to be vulnerable with Sonny

and that felt good. It had been a long time since I felt that way with a man and he reminded me that it's possible. I want more of that. I saw the importance of trusting myself, and defending myself, when I need to. Knowing my truth, I am guided to speak up. It feels powerful. And I can do so with kindness and confidence.

The biggest gift from the short time we had spent together was that Sonny helped me see how beautiful I am inside and out. Ever since high school, I did things so he would notice me; he said he always had seen me. I was the one that couldn't see myself as beautiful as he did. Now, I no longer felt the need to be seen or heard by him. I didn't feel the need to be someone who tried to fit in. I was finally able to be myself and love myself as I am.

I practiced all that I had learned from my coaching and I also incorporated other tools that I learned along the way. I was clear about what I wanted and didn't want. I now know that the love always remains even if the relationship ends. Sonny and I keep in touch now and again. Our love connection will continue forever. That feels precious.

The same week I completed my coaching program with Rochelle, Tommy showed up again at my door. I had no intention of ever speaking to him again and he knew it. That's exactly why he showed up. As I was walking to the door to answer it, I knew it was him. I felt a flood of power extend throughout my body. It was a wave of fire lighting me up and there was no fear present at all, just determination. I was ready and I knew it! His initial reaction was to back away and put his hands up to signal defeat. I reminded him that he was not welcome at my house nor in my life ever again. I shut the door and he left. My heart was pounding; I was shaking. And yet I felt relieved and powerful all at the same time because I was very proud of myself.

For years after, Tommy continued to reach out but I never responded. I am grateful that he showed up in my life for many reasons. He shook me and woke me up so I could take the action to change. I saw how I was settling and not speaking up for myself. Many of the things I did and I put up with were far out of alignment with my integrity. I went from being myself to becoming someone I was not, just so I could be in a relationship. I lost myself. Never again!

Looking back now, I can see how my heart was connected to both of these men. The way I felt with them was as though we had known each other for many years and beyond. I was able to be myself and feel accepted and loved. My heart truly knew theirs. Yet if my power and strength are missing in the connection, I know it is not a long-term relationship for me. Now, I have become clear and very discerning about not only the men in my life, but all relationships. I go along with the ones that bring me delight. I am more mindful and honest with myself. There is more harmony in my life, more bliss. I have a better relationship with myself. I have learned to open my heart and trust its guidance most of the time. When I do, all is well.

SHE FEASTS WITH HER ANCESTORS
TO GROW AND LOVE AGAIN

By Lady Beltane

On my dark days, I still wonder why my parents were taken from me at such a young age. My father was a young man of 36 and I was only 12 years old when he passed in 1970, so it was just me and my mom until I was married for the first time at age 16. I had a stormy relationship with my mother for many years, but when she died in August 2015, I lost one of my best friends. I sat with her in a coma for 20 days, never leaving the hospital. My head was glad she was through suffering, but my heart was broken.

My relationship with my mom was difficult for many years because I was rebellious as a teenager, and even into my thirties. My mother and I fought a lot, which included me calling her some very unpleasant names. I saw things, such as child rearing, in a totally different way than she did, and this caused many clashes between us, especially since she helped raise three of my five children. But my mom always had my back, no matter what I did or said. She was there to live with me when my marriage broke up and I had five young children to care for, in addition to working full time. If not for her, I don't know how I would have made it through those years.

During this time, I got into drugs at one point and was drinking very heavily. Instead of my children being taken away from me to be put in the foster care system, my mother took guardianship of them. This period in our lives was the worst one we went through in our relationship; we did not even talk for almost a year, even while she was living with my children and I lived with my boyfriend. For a period of time, she would not even let me see my children unless she was there because my temper was, admittedly, a little out of control. Her first instinct was to always protect her grandchildren.

After my children were grown and on their own, my mother and I worked things out by talking about all of our problems from the past in a civilized manner instead of shouting at each other. These healing conversations took place over a couple of years as we met for meals and coffee. We came to the conclusion to let the past be the past, and look to how we wanted our relationship to be going forward. She then became one of my best friends. I could talk to her about anything and everything.

Her funeral was a nightmare for me. I had to almost be carried away from her and my father's gravesides. I was devastated by her loss and went into a deep depression, not leaving my bed for days at a time. I cut myself off from the world. Even through all the sorrow, depression, and isolation, I never lost my connection to The Craft, nor my faith that the Goddesses and Gods I work with were around me, trying to comfort me through the darkness if I would let them.

The Craft was handed down to me in little ways through my family matriarchy; specifically, my paternal and maternal great-grandmothers and my mother. While we did not come together to celebrate Full Moons, or do spells, or do anything else as a family coven, they taught me invaluable practices for becoming the witch I am today. My great-grandmothers taught me how to use herbs to treat illnesses and how to gather them at the right time in the Moon's cycle for them to be the most potent. My mother taught me that the "voices" in my head were actually people, either Earthbound or in the Summerlands, trying to connect with someone on the physical plane. I resonated with these teachings of The Old Ways, including the understanding that everything has a dual nature of masculine and feminine. I was comfortable recognizing and embracing not only Gods, but Goddesses as well, and the good I could do with a spell or the right mixture of herbs. I came to The Craft and The Old Ways because I could be myself and not get criticized for doing it my way, which was, unfortunately, my experiences in the many other faiths I tried to fit into.

One night, I was alone and crying over not ever hearing my mother's voice again. Then all of a sudden, as clear as a bell ringing on a windy day, I heard her say, "Do not grieve so hard for me as I am happy here with your daddy, brothers, and sisters." After talking with my mother in the Summerlands, I felt more at peace with myself and her crossing over. For the next couple of days, I replayed in my mind what she said to me. Each time, I was elated to hear her voice again as I was missing that part of her more than anything.

That same night when I heard her voice, I had a dream, or possibly travelled to another plane, and I saw my entire family gathered together: parents, seven siblings, grandparents, great grandparents, and so on back throughout time. They were all sitting at a long table laid with a magnificent feast. There was an empty chair at the right hand of my oldest male ancestor. I asked who the empty chair was for, and I was told by my mother that when I visit them in my dreams or meditations, this was a place for me. I was also told I would only be able to sit in it for short periods of time until my time came, many years from now, to join them permanently in the Summerlands.

It is hard to put into words the awesome beauty of the Summerlands. The closest I can come to a description is to picture a beautiful summer day just after a light early morning rainfall: the fresh air; the damp grass, soft under foot; the birds singing in beautiful voices that sound like Angels' songs; and the sun shining so brightly it is almost blinding. One of the main things I brought back from my initial trip to the Summerlands was feeling more of a connection to Mother Earth than ever before. When I woke up the next morning and went outside to sit in the grass for my morning meditation, I could actually feel my ancestors around me, and my mother and father holding my hands during the quietest part of my meditation. This is something that still happens to me if I sit in meditation and allow myself to open up to them.

Slowly, I started coming back out of my shell after my mother died. The cures for my heartbreak have been a lot of meditation, friends writing to check in on me, and my children and grandchildren showering me with love and lots of prayers. I still have periods where I feel her passing as if it happened today. The only way through these times is by turning to my faith, family, and friends. I also remember the family feast in the Summerlands and being a part of that gathering. It is something I cherish and look forward to. I then continue following my spiritual path and living life with a heart full of love, hope, and positive energy. If I lose those things, I meditate and quickly feel surrounded by the love of my ancestors and siblings, which gives me the courage to keep going and to help others when I can. My mentoring of Novice and Adept level witches also helps to occupy my mind and allows me to learn new things, not only on my own spiritual path, but about The Craft as well.

It brings me great comfort to know that my family is watching over me and mine as Guardian Angels. I grow stronger each day in the love and caring of my ancestors, even if they are not here in the physical.

SHE GRACEFULLY LETS HER MUM GO

By Sass Jordan

My Mum died October 24, 2015. There was nothing spectacular, loud, dramatic, or lurid about it. She waited until I had left town to work for two nights, and then she died in the morning, right before I had to get on a flight to come home. She left the way she lived the last 20 years of her life: quietly, in a bright, clean space with kind, attentive helpers, and in relative peace.

Strangely enough, her granddaughter, my daughter, was more of a midwife to her death than I was because she was able to spend more time with her than I could. My daughter was the most wonderful partner in the process of dying. She would read to my Mum; lay with her in bed; helped her to drink water; and took her outside in the wheelchair to feel the remains of summer on her skin.

Before her passing, I was in a state of emotional yo-yo, which is a profound experience consisting of slamming up against the waves of grief, fear, and fury, and then falling helplessly into the troughs between the swells. The troughs between the waves are a strange mixture of suspended animation and surrealism as you realize that these towering waves are made from the ocean of your tears. I have never cried that much, or felt so helpless, while at the same time trying to hold up a front so that my Mum wouldn't feel badly about leaving. I didn't want to mar her exit in any way, or discourage her from finally making the journey she had been looking forward to for longer than I could remember.

My Mum was not a fixture throughout my adult life. We had a long period of no real communication other than letters sent snail mail across the Atlantic Ocean during the 1980's, and for a bit in the 1990's. She had moved back to England, where she was from, after she and my dad divorced in the early 1980's. She and I had only reconnected when my husband and I brought her back to live near us in Canada in 1999, a year after my daughter was born. She was in our lives regularly for the next 16 years; a wonderful, eccentric, funny, sweet, and intensely loving being, whom I shall never forget— never, ever, ever.

Mum and I could talk about everything. She told me my first dirty joke; there was nothing that was off-limits with her. I was one of the loves of her life. In her eyes, I was pretty much the greatest person who ever lived. I mean, she could get pissed off at me, and she did, but it never lasted. She always forgave me, and she was always there to defend me, although she often said she didn't really understand me. She always told me I was one of the most beautiful women she had ever seen, and that I was bold and courageous and funny and smart and super talented. She told me she came from a different time in history and that she didn't quite understand how it worked now; that her time here was over. She would ask me what she was still doing here when she was feeling especially superfluous in our society, which came more frequently towards the end of her life. I would tell her that she was still here because obviously she was still making a difference in other people's lives. Pretty much everyone that met her loved her. She was a spiritual mentor to many, many folks.

My Mum is the person who first made me aware of spirituality, of there being a language we could use to describe worlds and ideas beyond those that we could see with our physical selves. She is the first person who ever spoke to me about reincarnation, of the possibility of there being more than just this body, of the existence of God, of something greater than ourselves. My Mum taught me compassion and giving, and the fact that sometimes all people need is a good hug. She wore a winter coat on which she had stenciled "PEACE TO THE WORLD" in her handwriting on the back. She hugged random people wherever we went: supermarkets, restaurants, farmer's markets, malls. And when asked why, she would reply, "They just needed a hug".

I was terrified of her dying. Terrified of her not being here, terrified of having to go on knowing I couldn't talk to her, hug her; hell, just see her. She herself was NOT terrified of dying. In fact, she was kind of looking forward to it and would talk about it regularly, much to the chagrin of the people around her. She talked me through a lot of it, and she let me cry without stopping me or making me feel bad.

The last car ride we took together from her apartment to the hospice was one of the most difficult things I've ever done, because I actually knew we would never take another car ride together in this lifetime. I had to reach down pretty far into the bravery banks to deal with that one.

The time my Mum spent in hospice was a sacred passage for her, and for us, her family. She was absolutely delightful with the staff and they all naturally loved her. She was funny as heck, too. She had a friend who owned a farm with a bunch of animals right down the street from the hospice. One day, her friend decided to bring a donkey with her to say hi to my Mum. Don't you love someone who brings a damn donkey to a hospice? There was a sliding door from Mum's room that looked out over the gardens. The friend was trying to bring the donkey into her room, so that Mum could pet it, but it didn't really want to go inside the room. Mum just looked at the donkey, looked at her friend, and said, "Get your ass out of my room."

Facing the death of someone you love deeply is related to facing your own death in certain ways. You know you will never be the same person you were before they died. The fact is, we are never the same person anyway. It is just that death, in its apparent finality, tends to bring the emotions of loss and abandonment to the fore of one's consciousness. Who knew those little fuckers were buried in there, in all their itchy, burning, scabby, aching glory? Part of the road to healing and forming scars over the wounds is dealing with the scratchy regrowth of new skin tissue. Healing is uncomfortable and very often messy. It's a hell of a ride. The extraordinary thing about these types of tsunami-style life experiences is that they leave you with really no other alternative but to find a way through. Either that, or you basically die, too.

I had to find a way to live without that wonderful, unconditional love that would beam out from my

Mother's eyes whenever I was feeling under the weather, ugly, useless, uninspired, unappreciated, or any of the gross things that we humans spit up from the depths on bad days. I had to move through it all without her. Taking the time to cry and let out the anguish that strangles our hearts helps immensely. Spending time on my own, reading books from spiritual teachers, reading the works of Hafiz, Mum's favorite poet, and giving love in whatever way I can back to the world has been a source of personal healing.

To be frank, I think her passing has brought me to a new understanding of myself. It is as if she took the old, impatient, childish me with her. I mean, those parts are still there, but they are tempered with a greater self-love, one that is threatening to maybe even erase those immature parts eventually. I have more patience and kindness with myself, and more acceptance of the idea of my own death. Perhaps I have internalized the love I received from her because she is no longer here in person to give it to me. It is odd, but the strength of character that I feel that I have gained from her dying is empowering.

Is she still with me? Some days I think she is, and other days I do not. I have never gotten 'a sign' or a message that I could identify as coming from her. I feel like she is off on a spectacular adventure right now, and she'll send word when she gets a moment.

For now, I just move forward and send kisses whenever her essence makes itself known in my heart.

CLOSING THOUGHTS

When we experience the worst of times, we also have the opportunity to experience the best in ourselves. We never even knew these parts of ourselves existed until we are pushed to go deeper into our inner world to find new wisdom and higher truths. Life invites us into these hidden realms through struggle, challenge, fear, and pain. And when we are brutally honest with ourselves about our feelings and unconscious parts, we can voyage into those darker terrains with the light of our own soul leading the way.

The hardest work we may do in life is surviving the pull down into our own darkness, shadows, and fears. But this is also how we become truer, more authentic versions of ourselves. Open up to the invitation to release a story, a perspective, or a limitation so you can move forward to create a new, higher understanding of your potential and possibilities.

Perhaps you are wondering—or maybe you have completely forgotten—what happened to our dear young Persephone? (Quick recap: she was picking flowers in a lovely field and was suddenly kidnapped by that stinky monger Hades, who took her into the yucky Underworld due to her beauty and charms. He saw her light and he wanted to own it.)

Thankfully, Persephone's mom, Demeter, had her back. Demeter was the Goddess of Fertility and Harvest, and when her daughter was kidnapped, she withheld her power, too. Demeter searched high and low for her beloved Persephone, and vowed to not produce another healthy harvest of grains, vegetables, fruits, or anything else on the earth until her daughter was rightfully and peacefully returned to her. Humanity suffered while Demeter combed the lands for Persephone.

Meanwhile, down in the Underworld, Persephone refused to eat while in Hades' den. The poor lady was hungry, of course, but she had no desire to cooperate with the likes of him. Instead, she focused on observing his unconscious ways, understanding the darkness more, witnessing what the Shadow World was like, and emoting her fears and deep feelings in private. Finally, out of desperation, she ate some pomegranate seeds that Hades gave her, yet she did not understand what eating food from him meant for the long-term. It turned out that any food that was consumed from Hades was also a commitment to live in the Underworld with him for eternity.

Persephone was outraged!

And her mama was not having it. Demeter negotiated with Hades for her daughter to return to the world of light and sunshine for half of the year, while also maintaining her commitment to be with Hades for the other half of the year. Hades agreed. Persephone would go down to the Underworld during the fall and winter when the earth was barren, and then her mother Demeter would prepare the land with fresh flowers and bright greenery for her return to the light in the spring and summer. With this compromise in place, Demeter allowed the harvest to finally return, the flowers bloomed once again, and the earth's natural resources produced their bounty.

The Greeks perceived Persephone's voyage to the Underworld, and each annual return to the earth, as the reason for the change of the seasons every year. Since the Greeks could not use Google to research any other type of explanation, we'll just let them have their understanding.

Now, it would be understandable to feel sorry for Persephone in some way and think she was a victim for what she went through—but she doesn't need that perspective because, in fact, the opposite is true. When she came back up from the Underworld, Persephone was a new woman; a more powerful, mature version of herself than the innocent, simple girl who only knew goodness and light. She became the only Goddess who could successfully take others into the Underworld, the Shadows, and the darkness, as Hades would not allow anyone else into his realm. She became a powerful guide who could assist others with their own rebirth into a new life and higher consciousness by showing them what they feared. Persephone moved from a naive, protected view of the world into a grander, all-encompassing understanding of life and human nature. The full spectrum of humanity was now available to her, and this access became her power and her purpose. She was no longer afraid of what she could not see because she knew she could go into it for deeper inspection and gifts.

As these 24 women have shared with you in their

stories, life is an ongoing journey of change and evolution of self into a more expansive understanding of your inner world and unconsciousness. You make your life what you want it to be. You have the power and choices to do so. You have more strength, confidence and healing ability within yourself than anything outside yourself could match. What may at first appear to be a devastating yank or downward spiral into the darkness by a cruel life development could also be your voyage into greater light. This journey may be unexpected, shocking, difficult, and really hard, but you have the resources, teachers, guides, and insights to keep going through it all.

Just as these 24 women shared, you become more of yourself *because* of that experience.

Then you will re-emerge back into your own light with more strength and confidence in yourself than ever before.

Collective wisdom from these stories to take with you:

- Say hello with true openness to whomever shows up.
- There is a life-changing power in moving to a new location.
- Hearing a Voice, an internal message, a whisper, or an idea that isn't from your own brain can be exactly what you need, so pay attention to it.
- Acceptance and allowing, plus releasing resistance and opening up to surrender are ongoing, continual daily practices.
- Your deepest journey is more internal than external.
- Trust in the Divine/God/Spirit/Source—whatever that means to you—and in whatever way that has value to you.

- Look for life's invitations that nudge you forward to take a chance and try something new that calls to you.
- Stay open to your true feelings even when it may be very tempting to shut them all down and look at a handheld device.
- Let yourself off the hook at times because you are only human - and need to give yourself a break.
- Find simple joys and peaceful places to rest along the way.
- Say goodbye with gratitude and love.
- Never give up on yourself because your soul is always calling you forward.

Onwards may you journey out,
down,
and back up to the light.

"She transforms her own dark into her own light.
She sees her private shadows — and loves them.
She meets her emotional depths — and owns them.
She faces her private fears of separation — and rises above the illusion.
She is the source of her Self and she is always in a state of greater becoming."

The Modern Heroine's Journey of Consciousness

BOOKS WE RECOMMEND

Baughman, Alison. *Speaking To Your Soul: Through Numerology,* CreateSpace Independent Publishing Platform, 2013.

Byrne, Rhonda. *The Secret,* Atria Books/Beyond Words, 2006.

Coelho, Paulo. *The Alchemist,* HarperSanFransisco, HarperCollins Publishing, 1993.

Ford, Debbie. *Spiritual Divorce: Divorce As A Catalyst For An Extraordinary Life,* HarperOne Publishing, 2006.

Gray, John. *Men Are From Mars, Women Are From Venus,* Harper, First Edition, 1993.

Hardy, Diana "Dynasty". "Days I Haven't Known" from the album, *A Star in Life's Clothing.*

Hesse, Herman. *Siddartha,* Bantam Publishing, 1982.

McCord, Molly. *The Art of Trapeze: One Woman's Journey of Soaring, Surrendering, and Awakening,* Spirituality University Press, 2013.

McCord, Molly. *The Modern Heroine's Journey of Consciousness,* Spirituality University Press, 2013.

Newton, Michael, PhD. *Journey of Souls: Case Studies of Life Between Lives,* Llewellyn Publications, 1994.

Plant, Tamara. *Forgiveness And Other Stupid Things: An Awakening That Was Written In The Scars,* CreateSpace, 2016.

Rusch Watson, Laren. *WTF?! I Have Cancer? How to Get Through the Hardest Time of Your Life With Strength and Optimism,* Balboa Press, 2016.

Vitale, Joe and Ihaleakala Hew Len, PhD. *Zero Limits: The Secret Hawaiian System for Wealth, Health, Peace, and More,* Wiley, 2008.

Walsh, Neale Donald. *Conversations With God: An Uncommon Dialogue, Book 1,* TarcherPerigree, Penguin Group, First Edition, 1996.

Weiss, Brian L. *Many Lives, Many Masters: The True Story of a Prominent Psychiatrist, His Young Patient, and the Past-Life Therapy That Changed Both Their Lives,* Touchstone, Simon and Schuster, 2012.

Zukav, Gary. *The Seat of the Soul,* Fireside, Simon and Schuster, 1990.

ABOUT THE AUTHORS

Meet us here:
ModernHeroineSoulStories.com

She Begins Hearing Her Soul
Isabella Aponte is a Creative Writing teacher at a middle school in Philadelphia, Pennsylvania. This is her first published piece of writing. She plans to continue her passion for education and writing, by following wherever her soul may lead. Join her newsletter at http://eepurl.com/czGqOP

She Finds Her Power By Being Forced Into Battle
Alison Baughman is a professional Numerologist, author, lecturer and who has hosted Visible By Numbers, a popular weekly talk radio show about Numerology, on BBS Radio for over 5 years. Alison has been reading as a professional for over 16 years for people across the United States and Internationally. She is the author of "Speaking to Your Soul Through Numerology" and "Get His Number" both available on Amazon. www.VisibleByNumbers.com

She Blooms With Wisdom From a Friendship's End
Sharon Bright is a spiritual teacher. Her passion is to help lead women to fully accept themselves, by facilitating communities that encourage them to support and connect to other women. She is a wife, a mother, and a friend. www.sharonbrightlife.com

She Opens to the Power of Her Femininity
Alice Brooking is a lover of life and plant-based living. She has a wide range of interests, from alternative healing methods and astrology, to DIY home improvement. She is the proud mother of one beautiful boy.

She Feasts With Her Ancestors to Grow and Love Again
Lady Beltane is an ordained Pagan High Priestess who has been practicing The Craft for over 40 years. She lives in a suburb of Chicago, IL with her husband. Lady Beltane mentors novice and adept level witches through her website covenlife.co. She is also a mother and grandmother.

She Embraces the Gift of the Deer
Connie Cole, M.A., is a writer, a pipe carrier, an intuitive practitioner, and a champion of personal empowerment. An explorer by nature, Connie utilizes insights and skills garnered from decades of involvement as student and teacher with various practices of deep self-learning. She now draws upon these experiences and wisdom to assist others in their journeys of growth. www.connie-cole.com

She Surrenders to Not Knowing the Path Ahead
Erika Elmuts, is an internationally-recognized health and wellness expert, professional speaker and naturopath who has helped tens of thousands of people get on the path to more vibrant health through her workshops, television and radio appearances, website, videos, speaking engagements, and private practice. Erika is also the creator of the online course "The Cancer Prevention Blueprint" and author of "The Family Guide to Detoxing your Body and Home."
www.ErikaElmuts.com

She Opens Her Heart and Owns Her Power
Holly Faith runs her own business from Colorado. She enjoys spending time in the great outdoors and is currently following her passion of creating a space focused on community, acceptance, support and healing for all.

She Chooses Her Next Life Vision
Lauren Goldstein is a serial entrepreneur, speaker, author, igniter, and young-at-heart dreamer. As a maverick leader, she is the founder and CEO of Golden Key Partnership which specializes in the neuroscience behind Entrepreneurship and Business. You can discover more of her work at www.GoldenKeyPartnership.com.

She Unmasks Her Inner Magic

Hydee Hall lives in southern California with her husband Kevin who thinks her "woo woo" stuff is literally LOL funny but he supports her with unconditional love! Being a typical female Virgo, she is constantly evaluating herself to be a better version and explore life to its fullest in the absence of fear. After raising 3 boys, she feels she's really stepped into the adventure of connecting in depth to her soul and the synchronicities the Universe puts in her path.

She Rekindles Her Fire Within

Diana "Dynasty" Hardy is an international hip hop soul artist and youth advocate. She currently splits her time between touring and performing, and working with youth via her empowerment initiative, The Push Project. With a passion for the arts and a heart for youth, she is committed to helping others push for the dreams. www.thepushproject.org

She Follows Her Stars to Deeper Enlightenment

Dominique Jaramillo is an Astrologer, wife, mother and lover of all things mystical. She lives in Los Angeles, CA and enjoys teaching and guiding others with readings that inspire self-discovery, confidence and compassion. She is the creator of Conscious Astrology Wear for women and kids and you can learn more about her offerings at www.dualityandbeyond.com.

She Gracefully Lets Her Mum Go
Sass Jordan is a Juno Award-winning artist who has sold over one million records worldwide over the past thirty years. Sass was a member of the judging panel for Canadian Idol during all six seasons from 2003 to 2008. She has performed with Aerosmith, The Rolling Stones, AC/DC, Steve Miller Band, Van Halen, The Foo Fighters, Cheap Trick, Santana, Joe Cocker, Styx, Rodger Hodgson, April Wine, Jeff Healy, and countless others in her ongoing career. As an accomplished actress, Sass starred in the lead role of Janis Joplin in the off-Broadway hit, "Love Janis." www.SassJordan.com

She Takes Steps Into Her Inner Self
Debora Kiyono lives in Brazil. She loves nature, yoga, astrology, dance, music, movies, TV, and reading. By having this first essay published, she has discovered her new passion: writing.

She Dances Her Way Back to Happiness
Lili Krnic resides in Toronto. She spends as much time as she can doing the things she loves, including writing, dancing, traveling, and hanging out with her loved ones. Despite a few setbacks, she still believes in love and kindness and likes to seek out the beauty in life. She can be reached at lilikwrites@gmail.com.

She Rewrites Her Life With Ho'Oponopono
Teresa Leming is a former Self-I-Dentity through Ho'Oponopono instructor and former coordinator of IZI LLC as she studied directly under Dr. Hew Len. Teresa is a Reiki Master, Certified in Energy Healing, Akashic Record Meditation, Munay-Ki, The 9 Great Rites of Initiation & Shamanic Portal, Divine Light Rays, Aura and Chakra Healing. **www.beefreesoulproducts.com**

She Deeply Connects to Her Healing Powers
Christine Lisio is a Spiritual Healer, Transformation Coach, and Certified Intuitive Strategist who is currently supporting clients around the globe. She has received a Divine gift to work directly with Master Angelic Beings and the activation of a higher faculty tool allowing her to find the truth in matter. Christine is an Academy Master Teacher at The Academy for the Soul and a Certified Intuitive Strategist. Learn more at www.SolHealingLLC.com

She Evolves Into Motherhood
Molly McCord, M.A., is a bestselling author of ten books, intuitive business coach, astrologer, radio show host, and spiritual teacher who conceptualized this book project to support more women around the world. Over 50,000 copies of her books have been downloaded globally. Molly is an Ambassador for Women for Women International. She hosts spiritual growth and writing beach retreats in Florida, where she lives with her husband and son. www.ConsciousCoolChic.com

She Awakens to Her Soul's Talents
Lorraine Paul is a Private Banker based in NYC and proud mother of one. This is her first published essay. Discover more about Lorraine on Facebook and www.LPLoveAdvocate.com or send her an email at lorrainepaul1111@gmail.com.

She Finds Her Connection to the Universe
Tamara Plant is the founder of YouAreFIERCE.com, a community built on inspiring, elevating and connecting people who want to purge the negativity in their lives. She is an international award-winning author who incorporates Eminem's lyrics and angel messages into her writing and teaching. "Forgiveness and Other Stupid Things" was her first book and she's looking forward to the launch of "Trading for Dharma" in the fall of 2017. www.YouAreFIERCE.com

She Moves Closer to Loving Her Struggles
Huntress Maxine Thompson lives in the Western United States with her clowder of purry cats. She continues her journey of growth toward a blissfully manageable existence, serving where she can for the greater good. You can read more about her Hepatitis C treatment experience in her blog about it: www.huntressmaxinethompson.wordpress.com

She Learns the Beauty in Pain
Brenda Quintero-Lombardi is a native Texan, living in Merritt Island, Florida. She is a Realtor who enjoys helping people find their happy space (www.realtywithbrenda.com) and also help other women by sharing the Thirty-One gifts opportunity (www.mythirtyone.com/brendabqgifts). She loves to spend time with family and friends, go to Disney World, and try new restaurants.

She Faces Her Feelings of Failure
Devon Telberg is an Architect in New York City, and a developing writer on spiritual psychology subjects. She loves to use her architectural experiences as an opportunity to collaborate with others in visualizing new environments and manifesting them together. Her design thesis and research work include the topic of the experience of spirituality in architecture, and the integration of perspective between the spirit and the built world. www.devontelberg.com

She Heals With Pure Acceptance
Laren Rusch Watson is a board-certified Holistic Health Coach, Author, Speaker, and Organic Wellness Expert. Her recent book, "WTF?! I Have Cancer? How To Get Through the Hardest Time of Your Life With Strength and Optimism", chronicles her journey through a double cancer diagnosis and the invaluable life lessons she learned along the way. She writes regularly on her blog at www.larenwatson.com and is active on social media as Organically Laren.

CONTRIBUTE AND CONNECT

The Modern Heroine's Journey Beach Retreat

Deepen your spiritual growth and know more about your Modern Heroine Journey - at the beach!

Enjoy time in a charming beachside hotel in Cocoa Beach, Florida as Molly McCord guides you on a transformational journey of soul growth + beautiful healing + inner joy + deeper wisdom.

This full immersion experience unfolds over the course of 5 days as you listen, collaborate, create, express, and arrive at a new understanding of yourself as a Soul in human form. Feel beautifully supported in an interactive, moving, flowing journey of transformation — no sitting in a chair for days!

You will experience a personalized journey filled with group gatherings and silent solitude, conversation and reflection, gratitude and realization, peace and release, joy and LIGHT.

Molly will guide you to deeper connections, wisdom, and understandings of yourself, while also teaching more of the spiritual principles and understandings from the book, *THE MODERN HEROINE'S JOURNEY OF CONSCIOUSNESS.*

Learn more about this Beach Retreat:
https://www.mollymccord.online/p/modern-heroine-experience

The Write Beach Retreat

Calling all inspired writers + authors + wannabe authors!

Enjoy time in a charming beachside hotel in Cocoa Beach, Florida as you take your writing career to the next level with deep-dive workshops + realistic directions + practical guidance for putting your unique brilliance on paper.

Over the course of 5 days, you will have the space, encouragement, and practical guidance to develop your writing career based on where you are right now.

The Write Beach Retreat is a combination of big group workshops, small group intensives, solo writing time, Introvert Hours, and personalized one-on-one guidance.

Before arriving, you'll have a Pre-Retreat Introductory Session with Molly so she can ask you questions about your writing endeavors, and then tailor your Beach Retreat focus so you gain the most out of your time here.

Learn more about this Beach Retreat:
www.mollymccord.online/p/the-write-beach-retreat

MORE BOOKS BY MOLLY McCORD

The Art of Trapeze: One Woman's Journey of Soaring, Surrendering, and Awakening (Book One in The Awakening Consciousness Series)

The Modern Heroine's Journey of Consciousness (Book Two in The Awakening Consciousness Series)

The Unlimited Sparks of a Bonfire (Book Three in The Awakening Consciousness Series)

Conscious Messages: Spiritual Wisdom and Inspirations for Awakening

Conscious Thoughts: Powerful Affirmations to Connect with Your Soul's Wisdom

Your Awakening Self: Connect Deeply With Your True Evolving Soul

Conscious Digital Detox: A 10-Day Guidebook to Re-Treat, Re-Meet & Re-Turn to Yourself

The Thought That Changed My Life Forever

Caché Paris: A Guidebook to Discover New Places, Hidden Spaces, and a Favorite Oasis

FREE DIGITAL DOWNLOAD:
Free download available at
www.ConsciousSoulGrowth.com:

Guided By Your Light: Ridiculously Loving and Celebrating Yourself

Lightning Source UK Ltd.
Milton Keynes UK
UKHW021821150719
346203UK00027B/1226/P